DARK EDGE PRESS

DISTURBED WATERS

PAUL McCRACKEN

Published in 2022 by Dark Edge Press.

Y Bwthyn
Caerleon road,
Newport,
Wales.

www.darkedgepress.co.uk

Text copyright © 2022 Paul McCracken

Cover Design: Jamie Curtis

Cover Photography: Canva

A CIP catalogue record for this book is available from the British Library.

ISBN (eBook): B09NQH2KKN
ISBN (Paperback): 979-8-8106-2061-7

CONTENTS

For my mother, my first fan and harshest critic.

CHAPTER ONE

Daylight started to break through the forest. Slithers of its light kissed the edges of the thin tree trunks that stood like a silent wooden army. Birds tweeted and rustled as they took flight somewhere up in the canopy. But their songs were drowned by Kim's heavy panicked breaths as she stumbled her way through the forest.

Her fair hair was dirtied with mud, as were her clothes. Her skin-tight, light blue jeans wore some marks of her ordeal. They were ripped at her knees and shins, exposing some of her skin. Stains and blood smeared her white sleeveless top. She wore a thin cardigan that kept getting caught in branches and thorns in her desperate rush.

She had dried tears around her eyes and cheeks, despite the fact she was still sobbing. She was tired, hungry and weak, but she couldn't stop now. She couldn't allow herself to get caught.

He would know she was gone by now; he would be

hunting for her.

Her only hope now that she'd escaped was to find a road, a way out of the forest to find help.

She stumbled and fell but got right back up again.

The shadows on the forest floor began to recede as the sun got higher in the sky. Kim still hadn't managed to find a road or even a trail. The chill of the wind was attacking her. It was early April, and the heat of summer had still not arrived. The cold sent shivers up her back, and her legs shook in an attempt to keep warm in her thin jeans. She hugged the loose, flapping sides of her cardigan to her body and hunched her shoulders over as she trotted on.

Fighting exhaustion, she had slowed to a walk.

Had she covered enough ground to put enough space between herself and the man who had been holding her hostage?

Kim had no time to look for Olga before she fled. The window of opportunity was slim, and she'd had to take it. If she got help, she was sure she could save her friend in time.

Kim had no idea what the man wanted with her and Olga, but she knew it had to be something sinister.

After walking for what seemed like hours, Kim slowly lowered herself down against a tree trunk. She drew her knees in towards her chest and wrapped her arms around them, resting her head between her knees and shutting her eyes. She had reached her physical limit; she could go on no further.

She knew when she closed her eyes what she would see. The place where she had spent the last two nights flooded the front of her mind. It was so vivid; it was like she was right back there.

A weathered room where the paint was flaking off the walls. Gusts of wind howled through a small broken glass window with a metal guard mounted over it from the outside. The ground was rough; uneven concrete with what smelled like urine and old faeces in one of the corners. An old, torn, and ripped assortment of blankets was where Kim was expected to make her bed. It was no more hygienic than the floor. That's why she chose a spot by the wall, underneath the broken, barred window. On both nights, she had to sleep there.

The cold was bitter, but the blankets did not tempt her.

A joyous sound woke Kim from her daydream. She listened out again, hoping to hear it once more to make sure it wasn't just her mind playing tricks on her, letting her hear something she wanted to. But then it came again, the sound of children yelling playfully.

Kim got a renewed spark of energy at the idea of being saved. She got up and began to trace the source of the sound.

Some smells were so strong that they took Kim aback. The scents of colognes and perfumes hit her as she came to an opening in the trees.

In front of her was a caravan park and a small children's playground.

Kim started running towards the caravans, but just before she left the cover of the forest, she felt someone grip her from behind, pulling her back and close to their chest. One of his arms wrapped round her stomach, the other rested on her shoulder.

She could feel the heat of his breath on the back of her neck as he spoke. 'You're a sneaky one,' he whispered.

He rested his head alongside Kim's, looking ahead at the caravan park and tutted, 'So close, yet so far.'

Kim began to cry in defeat. She didn't waste her breath begging for him to release her; she knew it was futile.

The man reached across Kim's face and started to gently wipe the tears from her cheek.

'Shh, it's okay.'

Kim saw an opportunity, twisted her head, and bit into his hand as hard as she could. The man cried out in pain and his grip loosened.

He immediately stepped in front of her, stopping her from running out from the trees towards the caravan park. Kim turned and started to run back into the forest. She didn't get far when she heard his thunderous stomps snapping branches on the forest floor right behind her. He tackled her to the ground, applying all his weight on her spine.

'Bitch,' he muttered, as he started to bind her arms behind her back with some cable.

CHAPTER TWO

Over the last four months, Carter had been chasing Ryan Platt's shadow but had so far turned up nothing. Ryan's identity was confirmed early in the investigation, after he'd previously been a suspect in another case. His DNA got linked with clothing he had discarded. The clothing belonged to women who had recently gone missing. Ryan had since vanished.

The women who'd disappeared were all in their early twenties. Only three of the seven bodies, believed to have been linked to Ryan Platt, had been recovered. All of them were found in water: lakes and rivers all around Ireland. Because of that, the press had branded Ryan 'The Fisherman'.

Carter's latest lead had led him to a known car thief, Dennis McCormick. He had a string of convictions, but nothing that Carter felt made him a threat. A warrant had been arranged to carry out a search of his home and take him into custody.

He drove down to McCormick's house. It was in a

run-down council estate in west Belfast. The area was notorious for its high crime rate. Even as Carter drove through the area, the bleakness was clear. Walls were dubbed with graffiti, there were numerous scorch marks on both the roads and the footpaths from previously lit fires and children ran wild through the streets. Some even threw stones at the car as Carter passed. The gates that lined a local community centre were rusted, with its paint flaking off. In an alleyway that separated two houses was a mountain of rubbish: bin bags, toys and a fridge.

Belfast was far from the city that once made headlines around the world with war raging on the streets. The city had become a player on the world stage for technology as well as the film industry. Regeneration and gentrification were still scarred however, by the past, that lingered within the communities' minds.

McCormick's house was deep in the housing estate. It was somewhere the police were not welcome, and it was no secret. Carter knew that McCormick had probably already been alerted to his presence by the locals, who looked out for their own.

There was a large gathering of youths on the street corner, drinking.

Carter parked up outside his target's house, where a squad car was parked.

He got out of his car and went over to the squad car. He tapped on the roof before lowering his head down to the driver's window. 'You ready?' he asked the officers inside.

The officers both nodded, opening the doors and

getting out.

Carter led the way to McCormick's front door and knocked on it.

The crowd of youths walked down the street and gathered just beyond the garden gate to get a good view.

'Should we check the alley around the back?' one of the officers suggested, just when the door creaked open.

A worn and tired-eyed Dennis peeked through the gap in the door. He was in his mid-twenties with a shaved head, and he had a grey tracksuit on.

'Peelers!' he heard the crowd of youths call out.

Dennis's eyes widened.

Carter put his hand on the door to stop it from closing.

Dennis reacted quickly, slamming the door, catching Carter's hand in the frame which stopped it from latching.

Carter cried out in pain before shoving the door wide open to reveal Dennis running to the back of the house.

'Go round the back!' Carter instructed the two officers, as he gave chase to the kitchen where Dennis had somehow locked himself in. Carter guessed that he'd wedged something up against the door from the other side.

Fearing that he would lose his man, Carter kicked, banged, and shoved the door until it started to edge open. The door split and fell apart until the gap was just wide enough for him to fit through.

As he began to manoeuvre through it, a loud hissing

noise was accompanied by a grey smoke that shot out into Carter's face. His eyes and throat began to burn, causing a fit of coughing. When the smoke cleared, he saw Dennis with a small fire extinguisher in his hands. Dennis came at Carter with it, swinging it wildly. Carter managed to grab hold of the extinguisher and wrestled it from Dennis while still stuck in the doorway. Now unarmed, Dennis ran out of the kitchen and into the back garden through another door.

Carter chased him outside where he was greeted by an empty unkempt garden. The grass was ruined, it was filled with huge craters and very little greenery had been able to sprout from the dried-up turf. There was a small collection of rusted bikes that were leaning against the tall fence that enclosed the garden. A small wooden shed sat in the far corner, which seemed like the obvious location for Carter to search.

A tower of bin bags rested against the side of the shed, almost reaching the height of the window that was covered in spider's webs from the inside.

Just as he reached the shed door, Carter heard the creak of a gate swinging open. He followed the sound to the side of the house where he spotted the gate closing. Carter gave chase again, swung it back open, and spilled out onto the street.

When he reached the front of the house, he heard the youths shouting encouragingly. Their heads were turned to the other end of the street, beyond them, Dennis was running up the middle of the road.

Carter broke into a sprint after him, with his blazer flapping in the wind. The youths erupted in taunts as he rushed past them.

Carter started closing the gap fast, Dennis noticed too after a glance over his shoulder. He turned into another street, towards the back of the houses, and disappeared from view again.

Carter couldn't afford to lose him.

He turned the corner then came to a sudden stop.

On the ground in front of him, Dennis had been pinned face-down on the road by the two officers. One of them held Dennis and the other rose to their feet, handing something over to Carter. He glanced down and saw that it was a small kitchen knife. 'He had this on him,' the officer said.

'Bag it and arrest him,' Carter said.

***

Carter entered the interview room where Dennis was already seated.

It was a grey, empty room with bleak, solid walls, a small window allowing in just a slither of daylight, a table and chairs, and a camera on the ceiling to visually and voice record the interview.

Carter took a seat opposite Dennis, who wore an unconcerned look on his face as he slumped into his chair.

'So where did you get the car?' Carter asked.

'What car?' Dennis asked, playing dumb.

'Blue Honda Civic.'

'Don't own one,' Dennis replied.

'You don't own any cars but that hasn't stopped you getting caught driving a few.'

'I'm entitled to have some sort of legal aid here,

yeah? I think I'll exercise my right to remain silent,' Dennis said, smiling and folding his arms.

'You can do that. But I'd love to know how your solicitor will get you out of this one,' Carter said. He stood up, taking a seat on the other side of the table, sliding it right next to Dennis before sitting down again. He continued. 'Don't worry, you don't have to talk, let me just get you up to speed. You watch much news lately? If you do, then you will have heard of The Fisherman. He's been abducting and killing women for the last four to six months. The missing women's bodies haven't been found yet. The media have dubbed him The Fisherman because those bodies that have been found were dumped in the water, in lakes and rivers.'

Carter paused for a reaction, but Dennis remained tight-lipped, avoiding eye contact.

'Three days ago, two young women disappeared after leaving their night class in the college at around nine o'clock. We traced their movements as they made their way towards the city. You know what we found strange? This blue car kept on passing them, almost as if they were being followed. They haven't been seen since. We picked up an image of the car an hour later in north Belfast with you in the driver's seat.'

'Wait!' Dennis protested, his smug smile vanishing fast.

'It's okay, that's all. Just need to wait on your solicitor, I'll go and make sure the call is made,' Carter said, getting up and going to the door.

'Wow, just hang on there, mate. Chill a second, yeah?' Dennis said, just as Carter's hand reached the handle of the door.

'I am chilled,' Carter said confidently.

'Can we cut a deal? If I tell you about what went down?'

Carter walked back to his chair. He spun it round and sat down, leaning his arms forward over the back of it. 'I'm all ears.'

'I have nothing to do with the women's disappearances. But if I tell you what I know, can I walk?'

'Depends how good the information is,' Carter said.

Dennis took a second to compose himself before speaking, using a lot of hand gestures to explain his story. 'I just stole the fucking car, for a quick spin. I didn't follow any women. I never did anything to anyone. I wasn't in that car at nine!' His speech rose in speed.

'When and where did you get it?' Carter asked.

Dennis took a moment and began to speak again, slower and more contained.

'It was closer to ten. It was parked under the bridge on the road to the SSE Arena.'

'Then what happened?'

'No one was around. Place was dead so I smashed in one of the windows and got to work starting it. Took her for a spin. Followed the motorway and eventually ended up in Carrickfergus. On the return journey, I drove up to Cave Hill. That's when I started to poke around the car to see if there was anything worth stealing. When I got out and checked the boot, I knew I needed to get shot of the car.'

'What was in the boot?' Carter asked.

'There were a few things that just looked dodgy. A bundle of thick rope, a set of knives that were in a leather roll-up thing and two black bin bags. One of the bags had leaked on the floor, soaking into the fabric. I thought it was gonna be someone's head or something.'

'What was in them?'

'I only opened one. It had some clothes in it. I touched the bottom of the bag to see if it was still wet and it was a little. When I checked my hand, it was red, it was fucking blood mate! I took one of the dry pieces out and tried to use it as a rag to burn the car, but the lighter wouldn't work. The flint had broken or something, so I just got the fuck outa there.'

'Where is the car?'

'Maybe the same place I left it. The Cave Hill car park,' Dennis replied.

They were interrupted by a knock on the door. Carter got up and opened it. A pale young cop was standing outside. 'Chief wants you in his office – now.'

'What about?' Carter asked.

'Didn't say, just said to tell you to drop anything you're doing and get up there.'

'Right,' Carter said. 'Can you look after this one?'

'Hey! What about our deal?' Dennis protested as Carter left.

He made his way to Chief Paulson's office, which was on the second floor. He knocked twice before entering.

Chief Paulson sat behind his desk. There was someone seated in front of him. When the stranger in the room turned to face him, it was apparent that he was younger than Carter. He had the kind of baby-faced complexion that Carter had when he first made detective. His hair was shaved, and he had an air of smugness about him. It was on his face and in the manner in which he sat on the chair, slouched with one arm resting over the back of it. Carter knew Chief Paulson was a very formal person, which is why he was surprised that he had not corrected him.

'You wanted to see me?'

'Yes. Come on in and take a seat,' Chief Paulson replied, waving Carter in.

Carter closed the door behind him and took a seat.

'Carter, this is Liam,' Chief Paulson said, gesturing to the man in the chair.

Carter reached his hand over to shake Liam's.

'Hey.'

'Alright,' Liam replied.

'So, what's going on?' Carter asked, turning his attention back to Chief Paulson.

'Well, as you know, I'm still getting it in the neck from my superiors about producing results on The Fisherman case—'

'I've got a new lead,' Carter interrupted.

'We need more than leads now, we need results. Liam has just transferred from Newry with high recommendations.'

'Wow, wait a second. We both talked about this when I returned and started on this case. I don't want or need a partner on this. They will just get in the way and slow things down,' Carter protested.

'You don't trust anyone, that's your problem. Ever since you came back, you can't work with anyone without conflict or problems.'

'That might be because of the leaks this department has had,' Carter said. Then realising that he had started to raise his voice he brought it back under control. 'I'll admit I have a few trust issues because trusting others is what got me into such a mess before.'

'Can you give us a moment?' Chief Paulson asked Liam.

Liam got up and left the room.

CHAPTER THREE

ONE MONTH EARLIER

Today was the day.

Liam had arrived early with the rest of the team at the Newry headquarters.

Newry was a city that rested on the border separating Northern Ireland from The Republic. It was a city that also struggled against the same troubles that split Belfast. It wasn't quite as big as Belfast, but it contained a lot of manufacturing. The shopping centres at its heart attracted shoppers from as far as Belfast and beyond.

They had been tracking a group smuggling drugs into the country over the Irish border for the last few months. It was Liam's first case as a detective, under the watchful eye of his older mentor, Norman.

Norman was a bulky detective with short white hair and a well-trimmed white beard. He was known as 'Cheap Santa' throughout the department due to his appearance.

Liam was assigned to be Norman's partner four

months ago.

Norman had not held back his praise for Liam during their time together, impressed by Liam's fast-thinking and actions. To Liam, Norman had become like a father figure to him. Something that had been missing in his life since the death of his parents.

Norman was very old-school. Although he liked to do things by the book, he would try to achieve them by any means necessary, even if it wasn't a smooth ride. A straight talker, he was exactly the no-nonsense kind of mentor that Liam needed to keep him in check.

Liam met up with Norman in the locker room where Norman had already put on his tactical gear.

'You're late, kid,' Norman told him.

'I'm here, aren't I?' Liam replied, removing his coat, and opening his locker.

'You need to be *on it* today. There's no room for error,' Norman explained, straightening up.

'Don't worry, I'm ready,' Liam replied.

'I hope so, or it will be three months down the drain,' Norman said, leaving the locker room.

Liam regrouped with Norman out in the car park where members of the Armed Response Unit and the Tactical Support Group had gathered.

'Okay, now that everyone is here,' Norman said, looking to Liam, 'we believe our guys are coming to collect a cache in the Greenbank Industrial Estate. It's the warehouse that you were briefed about yesterday. Our guys are known to carry weapons, so use extreme caution and be ready for any situation. We try and take them peacefully but use force if you have to.'

Norman pushed Liam by the shoulder. 'This way.

We're riding together.'

***

Norman drove them deep into the industrial estate past the rows of factories and warehouses. The pathways were lined with cars and vans. Lorries and other large vehicles came and went, the estate was a hive of activity. There was a lot of noise from the passing vehicles, large ventilation systems of nearby factories and warning sirens. The tarmac on the road was broken with large potholes scattered along it. Every fence, that encased the grounds, they passed was an advertising board, each fighting for prominence.

Norman and Liam's car followed a police van in the middle of a convoy of marked and unmarked vehicles. They all kept a slow and steady speed, creeping towards their destination.

'This is it,' Norman said, indicating to turn right onto the grounds of a warehouse.

Norman came to a stop in front of the building.

Liam and Norman got out, following a group of officers making their way to the door of the factory.

The target building was one of the more recently built along the block, made up with fresh paint and shutters that were free from any dents or graffiti. It was a self-storage unit. Empty pallets were stacked against the perimeter fence, two branded vehicles were parked in front of the shutters and there was a freight container next to a loading bay. From the outside, it looked like a very reputable and legitimate business.

Norman and Liam drew their weapons as the officers in front of them breached one of the front doors into the building.

They stormed inside.

Liam followed the sea of officers as they flooded the modern offices through to the warehouse floor. A young female receptionist froze as the officers rushed through; Liam caught a glimpse of her face. She was young, maybe in her late teens. Her eyes followed Liam; he felt a certain sympathy for her. She didn't seem to have any idea of the kind of people she really worked for.

'Police!' numerous officers shouted out onto the warehouse floor with their weapons drawn.

The light inside the warehouse was dim, most of it entering through Perspex slots in the roof. The dust in the air was so thick that Liam could taste it on his tongue. Particles of it were visible under the beams of light filtering down from the roof.

In the middle of the floor, among the tall racks, were a group of men wrapping two large pallets. There was a small, weathered forklift next to them with a radio rested on its rear playing loud music.

The men were oblivious to the officers until the officers got closer when their warnings could be heard. Some of the men froze on the spot, while two started running to the far end of the warehouse.

Liam broke from formation, giving chase.

'Liam!' Norman called out after him, but he didn't stop. He knew he was going over Norman's head, ignoring his mentor's orders but he had a gut feeling that he had to make sure no one got away. With Norman being an older guy, Liam assumed he wouldn't have the stamina to chase them down on foot. The same might've applied to the other officers, he didn't know, but what he did know was that he could run like hell.

An officer ahead of Liam tackled the first fleeing man to the ground, but the other had made it to a fire door at the rear of the warehouse, swinging it open.

Liam ran as fast as he could, leaving through the fire door and catching a glimpse of the man at the top of the perimeter fence before he dropped down, out of sight, to the other side. It was the same kind of fence that Liam had scaled a million times before. Maybe not so much as a detective but certainly during his teenage years.

Liam launched himself up onto the fence and threw himself over it, landing on his feet on the other side.

The man looked back over his shoulder to see Liam chasing him. He turned his focus forwards again, dodging forklifts moving back and forth in the yard they were in.

Liam kept up the pace, weaving in and out of the forklifts, being shouted at by their driver's as he ran past. The yard grew loud with their protests, accentuated by the contemptuous *bleeping* of their horns. Liam kept his sight on the man ahead, he couldn't lose him. Especially not after going against Norman's call. He had no intention of returning empty-handed.

The man ran inside the factory through an entrance next to a large humming ventilation system. Liam followed him inside and ran through the main production floor which was filled with machinery and factory workers who looked at him in surprise and wonder. A worker dropped his tools at his workbench and tried to catch the man ahead, but he shoved the worker to the ground. Liam started to catch up thanks to the intervention that had cost the man ahead a couple of seconds.

They came out onto a loading bay. The man looked back at Liam again, who was almost upon him. The man held his chest and seemed to be gasping for air. He dropped down off a loading bay to the ground but stumbled, falling to the ground, and struggled to get back on his feet.

Liam jumped down from the loading bay and pinned the man to the ground. 'Gotcha.'

Liam radioed in his location and soon backup arrived, taking the man off Liam's hands and into custody.

Liam returned to the warehouse to find Norman outside. He was talking to a group of officers before he noticed Liam and walked towards him.

'We got them,' Norman said before a smile appeared across his face.

Liam and Norman embraced, patting each other's backs victoriously. It was strange for Liam to see a smile on Norman's usually stern face.

'Take the rest of the day off, get on home,' Norman told him.

'You sure?'

'Yeah, go on. I'll handle the paperwork. Besides, you have the longest trip home. How long does it take you to get back to Belfast?' Norman asked.

'Around an hour, depending on traffic,' Liam shrugged.

'Well get going. Enjoy it, you've earned it,' Norman said, going back towards the warehouse.

Liam took advantage of Norman's gratitude and managed to miss the usual traffic on his way back to his small house.

He couldn't wait to tell his sister the news. She had endured having to listen about the case – what he could tell her of it – for its whole duration.

Liam entered the house to the sound of the TV, which he found had been left on in the empty living room. The heating must've been on for a while, because inside, the heat was suffocating. The smell of lasagne hung in the air too. It was a favourite of Tina's. Liam couldn't stand it; he was a picky eater.

'Tina?' Liam called out, going up the stairs. He went to Tina's bedroom and opened the door to find her sitting fully-clothed on her bed, hunched up with her head hiding behind her knees and her dark hair.

'Tina, I—' Liam started, but then he caught a glimpse of what her hair was hiding. He leaned in closer and brushed Tina's hair away from her face. She was crying, her face was badly bruised.

'Where is he?' Liam asked angered.

'It's nothing, just leave it,' Tina said.

'Are you okay?' Liam asked, grabbing Tina's arm and checking it for further marks.

'Yes! Now just leave me alone,' Tina shouted, snatching her arm away.

Liam sprung up and walked out of the room.

'Liam?' Tina called in vain. Liam rushed down the stairs and out the front door. He got into his car, started the engine and sped out of the street with the engine roaring and his blood pumping.

***

Liam made the journey across town.

Tina had been in a relationship with the guy for around six months. Liam knew where to find his house because he'd collected Tina from it every other weekend. She knew that her new guy, Mike, was a deadbeat but that had never deterred her before. No matter what, Tina seemed to always end up with the wrong type of men. She was yet to find a good one. Of course, she wasn't going to take Liam's advice on the topic, he didn't expect her to, but he tried to convince her that these guys were not good enough for her, especially Mike.

Mike lived with his brother David.

Although Tina had been seeing Mike for so long, Liam hadn't yet come face to face with Mike or his brother. He'd only seen them in photographs, videos or as he waved Tina off from the porch before she got into Mike's car.

Liam finally found Mike's house, parked outside, and got out of the car and went straight to the front door. After he knocked, he forced himself to calm down and to steady his breathing. He took a few deep breaths and blew them out until he heard footsteps on the other side of the door. With any luck, they wouldn't recognize him, Liam hoped. It would make it easier with what Liam had planned.

The door opened to reveal a man with a close-shaved head. It was the brother, David. 'Can I help ya? Who are ya?' David asked.

'I'm a detective,' Liam said, flashing his ID. 'I was hoping to speak to Michael Johnson?'

'Mike! Cops are at the door for you,' David shouted back into the house.

Liam was in luck. The brother didn't seem to recognize him. Mike descended the stairs behind David and came to stand next to him.

'What's this about?' Mike asked.

Mike was in a tight black T-shirt displaying the tattoos that covered his arms in a sleeve and his neck. His hair was jet black and he had dark, thick stubble. It seemed to Liam that Mike hadn't recognized who he was either, which was perfect.

'I just wanted to run a couple of questions by you. If you want to step outside so we can talk, we can maybe sort this out here and now without having to go down to the station,' Liam said.

Mike looked at his brother then back at Liam. 'Uh, sure,' Mike said, stepping outside. Then turning to his brother, David, he said, 'Fuck off. I'll be back in a minute,' before closing the door. Mike followed Liam over onto the grass in the garden. 'So, what do you want to ask me?' Mike asked, rubbing his stubble.

Liam spun around and punched Mike in the face, knocking him down. Then, climbing on top of Mike he continued to punch him until his face was a bloody mess. He felt his fists hitting into the bones in Mike's face: nose, cheekbone, teeth.

The front door swung open, and David came rushing out of the house, tackled Liam till he sprung off Mike, and started kicking him.

Liam fought to his feet, taking blows from David as he did. David fisted the collar of Liam's T-shirt, ripping it as they struggled. Liam then grabbed the back of David's head and drove his knee up into his face twice before he fell on the grass next to his brother.

Liam staggered over to Mike, kneeling down next to him. 'Stay away from Tina,' Liam threatened.

Liam climbed back into his car. His clothes were covered in mud, and he could see grass stains on his knees.

In the rear-view mirror he saw one of his eyes was beginning to swell and bruise.

***

The next day, Liam received something of a hero's welcome at the station for closing the case. The activities of the night before had gone unnoticed to his relief. When he got home last night, he had started to worry whether Mike had reported the assault to get back at him.

He went to the kitchen and started to make a coffee. The kitchen was empty as he waited for the kettle to boil, reading what had been posted on the noticeboard.

'You're late!' Norman boomed, getting up close to Liam before startling him.

'Fuck you, you're gonna give me a heart attack,' Liam said.

'Grab your coffee and follow me, got some big news for ya. What happened to your face?' Norman asked, taking notice of the bruising.

'Bad reaction to eyedrops, I think,' Liam lied.

Liam did as Norman said and was unsure how to feel about the 'big news'. Then he started to worry again about beating on Mike.

Was he in line for a disciplinary?

He followed Norman upstairs and into the man's office. 'So, what is it?' Liam asked, taking a sip of his coffee and trying to remain cool as Norman got comfortable behind his desk. Norman then picked up a file and threw it at Liam.

'What's this?' Liam asked, taking a look at it.

'Big job in Belfast came up. The Chief Constable has been actively seeking recommendations for a position they are recruiting for.'

'What?' Liam asked, confused. He began to look through the file.

'There were certain specifications. They wanted young blood. Someone flexible, with fresh eyes. They're trying to partner someone up with Joseph Carter,' Norman said.

'Carter? The guy who closed the Pyro Killer case?' Liam asked.

'Seemed a perfect fit for you. Plus, it's in Belfast. No more long commutes down here. It's a chance to prove yourself, kid. Don't waste it,' Norman urged.

'I don't know what to say.'

'You're welcome,' Norman smiled.

Liam could tell from Norman's smile that he had a sense of pride in the fact that his own apprentice had made such an impression on him and now seemed destined for bigger things. But Liam was honest when he told him he didn't know what to say. He didn't know how to feel about it. He was comfortable where he was. Settled. He knew what to expect every day working with Norman. Now all of that was going to be stripped away from him through no choice of his own. And it seemed the choice had already been made.

Liam didn't dare spoil Norman's proud moment by bringing up that fact.

CHAPTER FOUR

'It's no longer up for debate,' Chief Paulson said with a stern voice.

'Now I've to babysit *and* try to catch this guy?' Carter asked.

'Make it work. Liam's a bright kid. Give him a chance. Don't think of it as a burden. Think of it as extra help.'

Carter got up from his seat and left without another word. Upon opening the door out of Chief Paulson's office, he found Liam stood outside. Carter continued past him, and down the hall, with Liam's footsteps soon following.

Carter entered his office, going straight to his desk and sitting down, letting out a frustrated sigh.

The door to his office opened, and Liam entered.

'You're supposed to knock,' Carter said.

'Well, seeing as we're now partners, I suppose that makes this our office,' Liam said.

'Are you always a cocky wee prick? Or is this a

nervous thing?'

'No, it's pretty much my default setting,' Liam quipped. He shut the door, cleared documents off a chair and set them on top of Carter's desk before taking a seat.

'Let's just understand each other now before going forward,' Carter started. 'I run this show. You're here to assist me, not to make things harder. I don't want to babysit you. If you fall behind, catch up quick.'

'Is that your speech?' Liam asked. 'You should really rehearse it.'

'Are we clear?' Carter raised his voice.

'Yeah, crystal. I can keep up.'

'Good.'

'When I heard I was gonna be paired with you, I did some digging.'

'Is that right?'

'You don't intimidate me, Carter. Everyone talks about you as a hotshot detective after the Pyro case, but I want you to know that after reading up on everything that happened, and now meeting you face to face, I have to say, I'm not impressed.'

'I'm glad we cleared that up.'

There was an awkward silence that followed. Liam took a good look around the office. Carter wasn't one for putting up pictures of himself around his own office, nor things that celebrated himself in any form, such as newspaper articles or certificates. In fact, apart from a couple of painted canvases, his walls were quite bare.

Carter got to his feet. 'You drive?'

'Yeah.'

Carter retrieved a car key from his pocket and threw it to Liam.

'We're going for a spin,' Carter told him.

'Are you not meant to bring me up to speed on this guy we are chasing?'

'We'll talk on the way,' Carter said, leaving the office.

Liam followed Carter out into the corridor.

Carter started to talk as they walked through the building. 'Guy's name is Ryan Platt. We first became aware of him during the Pyro case. He was the top suspect on that case at one time.'

'What gave him away?' Liam asked.

'We caught him dumping the clothes of his victims. Ever since then, he hasn't shied away from taking the credit for his crimes.'

They came out into the car park and Carter stayed silent until they passed a couple of officers. 'He targets young women who are anywhere from eighteen to thirty years old. We've found no evidence of the crimes being sexually motivated. I actually believed him when he told me that he only wanted to be famous. I think that's his endgame.'

'You've talked?' Liam asked, surprised.

They stopped opposite Carter's car. 'Take us up to Cave Hill.'

***

Carter and Liam drove out to the beauty spot at Cave Hill Country Park. The park was on the hills that overlooked Belfast. It was a favoured location for photographers, hikers and tourists.

They took the back road that rose up into the hills to the car park.

The car they were looking for had been abandoned in a corner of the car park, taking up two spaces. A forensic team were examining the vehicle. Liam passed through a cordon and parked up. They both got out and walked over to the abandoned car.

Carter asked for the team leader on the approach. The forensic team leader started detailing what they had found.

'What about this?' he asked, raising up an evidence bag in his hand.

'A work jacket?'

'Doesn't seem like a brand. Has a name on the collar: J. Penn.'

'What else have you found?' Carter asked.

The team leader began telling Carter what they had extracted from the car. Amongst the items they'd discovered were shoes, gloves, a bundle of rope, a leather wrap that held two hunting knives and the two bin bags that McCormick spoke of. He also explained that they had found a bag in along with the spare wheel. Inside was a range of large knives, cable ties and rags.

***

They had been at the scene for some time now. Liam stood watching forensic officers continuing to sweep the car. Carter was standing at the edge of the car park.

Carter finished a phone call and walked back over to Liam. He caught Liam in a daydream. He was staring at the officers before Carter's presence snapped him out of it.

'They're checking the CCTV from where Dennis McCormick claims to have stolen the car. I have a feeling he was putting a dampener on our friend's plan. Maybe he took the car before our guy could get to work.'

'What next then?'

'I got an address for that jacket. Belongs to a company in Carryduff.'

'So, what are we waiting for?'

'It's almost four o'clock. I think this is one for tomorrow. So go home, take the rest of the night off, and I'll call you in the morning.'

'You not leaving yet?' Liam asked.

'You take the car back. I'll grab a lift with these guys when we are done.'

Liam nodded and got into the car.

Carter watched him leave and then started to look at the surrounding hills. He had the unnerving feeling that they were looking back.

***

Carter got home at eight o'clock under the final glares of sunlight. He left his keys on a hook in the hallway before entering the kitchen. He put the kettle on and got a cup of instant coffee ready.

He entered the dark living room and pressed a button on his landline phone. An electronic voice spoke as he drew the curtains. 'You have no new messages.'

Carter switched on two tall, standing lamps that lit the room. There was a long black coffee table in front of two leather sofas. Facing it was a modern gas fireplace with a surrounding mantelpiece. On the mantelpiece rested a series of photographs. The first was of Emily, his niece. She was his motivation behind tracking down the killer of his previous case, following her murder.

The second photograph was of his other niece, Kiera. Kiera's mother, Rachel, had made sure to keep Carter at a distance. Rachel still wanted nothing to do with Carter. He thought it might be for the best. So since then, he had become something of a recluse. It was, in fact, trust that had got Carter into so much trouble before. Because of that misplaced trust, the people that Carter cared about had suffered.

He knew he couldn't make the same mistakes or take the same risks with this case. He cut them off from his life, not wanting to place anyone else in danger.

He sat on one of the sofas in front of the coffee table. His laptop was on top of it. Carter opened it up and started to hunt through folders.

He clicked onto a downloaded video.

A woman with dark hair and a face with soft, round features appeared. She had shot the video using her laptop's camera. Her name was Ashley. Carter hovered the cursor over the play button icon, hesitating before clicking it.

'Hey, Carter. I tried calling, but I kept getting the answering machine every time. Either you're busy, or you must have a new number. Anyway, I just thought I would send you an update and say hi,' Ashley said, adjusting her hair and the camera.

'It's going really well here. Still getting used to it. I got a small apartment in the city centre. It's quite close to the Guinness factory. I get a three-day weekend, I didn't realize when I had the interview, but I only have a four-day working week. It suits me great because I can get out and do all of the touristy things around the city.' She smiled, then paused for a moment, and the smile slowly evaporated from her face. 'It would be good to hear from you. I hope you're doing okay. And uh . . . that's it. Until next time,' she said, and then the video ended.

Carter continued to gaze at the still image of Ashley on the screen. He thought about calling her, but it was too late for that tonight. He closed the laptop and stared blankly at the walls, trying to fight the thoughts of how he had missed her.

CHAPTER FIVE

Liam picked Carter up the next day, and they went straight over to the factory where the jacket was linked to, in the small village of Carryduff.

They pulled into the industrial estate and parked up outside the building. Carter and Liam got out of the car and started walking along the path towards the reception.

'Let me ask the questions,' Carter insisted.

'Knock yourself out, boss,' Liam mocked.

Carter led the way into the lobby. The sun crept out from behind the clouds, and the entrance burst into light as they entered. The reception area had a brilliant white tiled floor with a glass coffee table surrounded by fabric sofas. A row of picture frames dotted the far wall that led down to a corridor. Carter could feel the warmth on his back as they reached the desk.

A small, thin lady with half-moon spectacles looked up and smiled when Carter caught her gaze. 'Hi there, how can I help?'

'I'm Detective Carter. This is my partner, Detective Harding. We need to look at your employment records concerning a case we are investigating.'

'Oh my, is it serious?' she asked.

'Well, yeah, it's a murder case,' Liam said with an attitude.

Carter looked back at Liam with a disapproving gaze before refocusing on the receptionist.

'I'll get the manager, one moment, please,' she said, picking up the phone at her desk and pressing a few buttons.

Carter walked into the middle of the lobby to wait, and Liam joined him.

'What was that?' Carter asked in a whisper.

'Sorry,' Liam apologized.

Carter settled himself, accepting the apology. 'It's okay. Just think, yeah?'

The manager reappeared after a few minutes. He was a chubby man with grey hair and a thick grey beard. His belly looked like it was ready to burst out of his pale blue shirt, followed by his navy trousers.

'Hey, detectives,' he greeted in a gruff voice, offering his thick, hairy hand out.

Carter and Liam took turns shaking it before getting straight to business.

'Hey, we need information on an employee, an individual called J. Penn,' Carter said.

'Follow me through to my office. I'll access the records there,' the manager said, leading them down the corridor where the picture frames were. 'Name's John, by the way.'

'What is it you guys do here, John?' Carter asked,

taking in his surroundings as they moved deeper into the building.

'We make glamping pods. You know the fancy outdoor camping shelters you see in holiday resorts?'

'Glamorous camping, isn't it?' Liam asked.

'That's it!' John replied, excitedly. 'Just in here.' John opened the door to his office.

Carter and Liam entered. Once inside, the first thing Carter noticed was an enormous whiteboard that spanned the entire length of the wall to their left. On it was various notes, from dates and numbers to technical information and small illustrations of what seemed to be parts of what they'd built.

John walked around them and sat at his desk, which was clear except for his large computer monitor.

'Right, what was the name?' John asked.

'J. Penn,' Carter said.

'Sorry there are no seats, lads. Upstairs have stolen them for a presentation.'

'No problem,' Carter said, turning to see what Liam was doing.

Liam was studying the whiteboard as well as the drawings that hung on the wall next to it.

'Here we go. Jamie Penn,' John said, gesturing for Carter to come around the desk to look at the monitor.

Carter walked round and looked at the screen. It showed an employee application form and a questionnaire.

'Do you remember him? When did he last work here?'

'He was on the night shift, so I would have only ever seen him leaving in the morning. One of our supervisors might be able to tell you, or . . .' John stopped, tapping a few keys on his computer. 'There,' he said, opening another document. It was a notice of resignation from Jamie Penn. 'Dated two months ago. Looks like you just missed him.'

'What was his reason for resigning? I can't make it out from here,' Carter said, standing over John's shoulder.

'His letter talks about another job.'

'Can you pull up his address?' Carter asked.

Carter left the building with Liam a couple of minutes later.

'We going to Penn's house?' Liam asked on the walk back to the car.

'Yeah. We still don't know who this guy is, so when we get there, watch your back.'

They took the short drive to the village of Moneyreagh. Along its small main road were a primary school, a shop, and a pub. It was a dense residential area. They arrived outside a series of newly built houses.

They got out and walked towards number three. Like the other properties, it looked clean from the outside, with a new brick design on the exterior, complete with a tidy patch of grass and a narrow-paved driveway at the front.

Carter knocked on the door.

'Looks like nobody's home,' Liam said after a few moments of waiting.

'You looking for Jamie?' a voice called out.

Carter and Liam looked into a neighbour's garden where a plump man stood locking his front door.

'Yeah,' Carter said. 'We're detectives. Want to ask him a couple of questions.'

'You'll probably catch him down at the lake. That's where he is on a Friday. He's always trying to drag me along.'

'What lake?' Carter asked.

'Do you know Loughbrickland?' the neighbour asked.

'No,' Carter said.

'Yes,' Liam cut in.

'Well, it's just off the carriageway. That's where he'll be.'

'Thanks, sir,' Liam said.

Carter and Liam got back into their car.

'You know where this place is?' Carter asked.

'Can't miss it, here,' Liam said, leaning over the dash. He began to operate the satnav. After a moment, he spun it, so the screen faced back at Carter in the driver's seat. 'There, it's punched in.'

According to the satnav, the lake was thirty miles south of Belfast. The last of the sunlight began to disappear over the horizon on their journey down; shadows growing larger on the road. The road fell into a mixture of twilight blue and amber, from the coloured lights visible from the houses that rested on the nearby hills. They joined the dual carriageway that led directly to Dublin. It was a busy road with long straights, and it cut down through the countryside of County Down with its rolling hills.

Carter and Liam bypassed the town of Banbridge, and a further few miles later, they saw a body of water.

They came off the carriageway before it bridged

over part of the lake. Carter stopped the car at the side of the small road that disappeared further into the countryside, and they both exited the car.

The lake sat beyond the trees that lined the side of the road. A slight breeze ruffled the leaves, with some of them breaking free from their branches. Carter scaled over a small wooden fence and went beyond the dense woods to see the entirety of the lake.

'So, this is the place?' Liam asked, catching up.

'Yeah,' Carter said, descending the field closer to the water.

'So, what now?' Liam called after Carter.

Carter stopped in his tracks to look around. The lake was huge, covered on all sides by grassy fields. In the middle of the lake was what looked like a grouping of trees, but it was hard to be sure if there was an island or not. The still water was only disturbed by some small birds that came and went. It was quiet. Only the nearby passing cars broke the silence.

'Is that a small hut over there?' Liam asked, pointing.

Carter looked at what Liam was suggesting. On the west side of the lake, near the water's edge, sat a small wooden building. In front of it was a boating dock.

'C'mon,' Carter ushered, leading the way over to it.

The ground around the wooden hut was muddy and worn. The grass became patchy and inconsistent. The hut's exterior was rotten and discoloured. Spider's webs covered the small glass window, and one of the metal panels that made up the roof swung and banged against another in the light wind.

Carter drew his gun, moving around to the front of

the hut. He heard Liam following him. Carter got in front of two tall wooden doors, where a slide bolt and padlock held them shut.

Liam cut off to the side of the shed and returned with a rusted spade. 'Watch out,' he said, as he stormed towards the doors with it raised above his head. He began repeatedly plunging it down, digging into the padlock and chipping into the wooden door. After a few strikes, the padlock fell off, and Liam unlocked the door. He gestured to Carter to enter first by bowing and extending his hands to the entrance.

Carter raised his gun and went inside. The loose roof panel kept banging in the wind. Carter took out his phone to use the flashlight. The shed had a strong smell of dampness, and piles of green fishing nets filled the floor. A workbench stretched along the wall at its rear, and on top of it was an assortment of junk: old coffee flasks, a pile of fishing magazines and some worn tools.

'Carter!' Liam's voice called from outside.

He turned off his phone's flashlight and went outside. Liam was waiting at the boat dock. A small rowboat rested on the far side of it. Carter went over to take a look.

He stood over the small boat, looking down inside it from the dock. It contained two oars. Carter knelt and carefully stretched one foot down into the boat. He climbed off the dock and landed inside the boat with both feet. He began looking around, under the seats, checking the oars and the water surrounding it.

'Look,' Liam said, pointing down towards Carter's feet.

'No, the side,' Liam said.

Carter hunched over to look at the hull and saw a message carved into the side of the boat.

Carter, go fish!

'What does it mean?' Liam asked, looking around. 'I don't see any fishing rods set up, do you?'

'There were nets in the shed. Maybe there is one set up out there.'

They both began to scan the lake, trying to spot anything on the water.

'Get in,' Carter said, lifting the oars.

Liam jumped down into the boat with no hesitation, which shook the boat more than it had when Carter had entered.

'Christ! Easy!' Carter said. 'I wouldn't trust this boat too much. Here.' He handed one of the oars to Liam.

They rowed out onto the lake, searching for anything in the water. Liam decided that they should row towards the trees in the middle of the lake. The trees began to tower over them as they got closer. To Carter, the look and sound of the leaves ruffling the water and blowing in the wind seemed eerie due to their isolation.

Carter and Liam passed under the branches, having to push some out of their way until the boat brushed against something.

There was a small island hidden beneath them.

Both Carter and Liam reached out, grabbing nearby branches to steady the boat and pulled themselves close to the island.

'I'm gonna look around. You stay here,' Carter said, as he stepped out of the boat and onto the island.

'Well, hurry up,' Liam said, keeping the boat in place by keeping hold of a branch.

Carter used the flashlight from his phone again to look around. It was a small island, maybe the size of a five-a-side football pitch. Tree trunks and roots made up most of the area, which Carter had to weave his way past to get to the other side. His shoes sank into the wet, muddy ground with each step. He got to the other side and looked out at the lake, but thickly leaved hanging branches obstructed his view. He checked the perimeter of the island on the way back, looking for anything out of place.

He finished his search, returning to the boat without a discovery to report.

'Anything?' Liam asked.

'Nothing here. Let's go back out,' Carter said, returning to the boat.

They rowed around the island to the other side of the lake.

Liam spotted something in the distance.

'Look, out there,' Liam pointed.

Carter stopped rowing, stood up and saw something orange floating on the surface of the water ahead of them. It looked like fishing net.

'Go,' Carter said, retaking his seat.

They rowed over next to it and stopped. Liam leapt out of his seat to grab it before they floated away.

'Got it!'

'Careful, let it go. We don't know what's inside. We need to call it in.'

'I can jump down and have a look.'

'Not a good idea,' Carter said.

'Why not? The worst case is it's some dead guy, isn't it? Feels like it. Won't freak me out,' Liam said, taking off his coat.

'Now wait, Liam!' Carter shouted as Liam leapt into the lake, sinking below its surface.

Carter began counting the seconds when all of the ripples from Liam's splash had settled. He started to wonder if he would have to go in after him. Bubbles started rising from the lake, and Liam came to the surface with a look of shock along with panicked breaths.

'What's wrong?' Carter asked, worried.

Liam pulled himself up into the boat and sat at its stern, hugging his chest with water dripping off his face that had turned pale.

'What is it?' Carter asked again.

Liam's jaw shook as he spoke, 'It's wrong, it's just wrong.'

***

The entire lake had turned into a crime scene that was now well-lit by floodlights; the darkness of the lake brought into the light for all to see.

Various officers helped bring the fishing net to shore.

Carter and Liam made sure they were among the first to see it.

Forensic officers placed the green net on a large white sheet. It was a tangled mess. The forensic officers were the only ones allowed near it to untangle it to reveal the body parts of a young woman.

Carter spotted Chief Paulson and made a beeline towards him. Chief Paulson was manoeuvring through various conversations until Carter grabbed his attention.

'Chief, a minute?' Carter asked. He began walking alongside him, with Liam following behind.

'This place would give anyone the fucking creeps,' Paulson said.

'Have they found out who she was yet?' Carter asked.

'We need to wait for a positive ID, but it could be the Madsen woman, the second last woman to go missing.'

'Wait, hang on, second last?' Carter asked.

'Yeah. A report came in just before I came down here. Another woman has been reported missing from this morning. So, wanna walk me through this?' Paulson asked, as they reached the doors of the wooden hut.

Forensic officers in white suits occupied the building, checking every surface and placing markers down.

'We came here on our follow-up of the jacket found in the stolen car we believe that Platt planned to use to hold up his next victim. We tried to reach the jacket's owner, but he wasn't home. One of his neighbours advised us he could be down here. So, Liam and I came here to conduct a search. That's when we found the netting out on the lake, which Liam dived in and found contained a body.'

'He okay?' Paulson asked, looking at Liam, whose

hair was still wet.

'He's already been checked by the paramedics.'

'Keep me updated,' he said, leaving Carter and Liam to speak to the others at the scene.

CHAPTER SIX

Carter arranged to pick Liam up from his house the following morning. It was a bright day with clear skies and a gentle breeze. He pulled up to the small house that was only half a mile from his own. Carter still lived on the outskirts of Belfast, close to the Ulster Hospital and the parliament building of Stormont.

Carter was surprised to find a young woman answering the door. She seemed to be around the same age as Liam, with dark brown hair tied up in a bun. She wore an excessive amount of makeup along with a bright coloured dress with loud patterns.

'Hey,' Carter greeted.

'Hello,' she greeted with a smile.

'Is Liam there? I'm here to pick him up.'

'Really? So, you're his new partner? He's told me a lot about you. Why don't you come in? He is gonna be a few minutes. He's still in the shower,' she said, showing Carter inside.

'Okay, thanks.'

He went into the small living room with the woman following.

'So, are you and Liam living together?'

'Yeah,' the woman burst into laughter after the question lingered in the air for a moment. 'Oh, not like that. He's my baby brother. Yeah, we're just house-sharing. I'm Tina,' she said, extending her hand to Carter.

'Joseph, everyone calls me by my surname, Carter,' he said, gently shaking Tina's hand.

'Can I get you coffee? Tea?'

'No thanks, just had a coffee before I left the house.'

'Tina, who was at the door?' Liam's voice shouted from upstairs.

Tina went out into the hall to shout back. 'It's Carter!'

'Shit, I'll be down in a minute!' Liam said, followed by a series of thunderous footsteps on the floor above.

'That boy will never change,' Tina said, returning to the living room. 'Go on, take a seat,' she encouraged Carter.

'So, what is it you do, Tina? If you don't mind me asking?' Carter asked, reluctantly taking a seat. He felt awkward, not just because he felt like he was intruding on Liam but also because his sister was attractive.

'Oh no, it's fine. I'm a makeup artist. Freelance really, I'm trying to start up my own business.'

'That's impressive.'

Thunderous footsteps rushed down the stairs, and Liam burst into the living room while putting on his coat. As far Carter was concerned, it was a welcomed interruption.

47

'Hey, good to go,' he said under heavy breaths. 'I take it you met my sister? Carter-Tina, Tina-Carter.'

'We've been chatting while you've been getting changed, you knob,' Tina said.

'Right. You parked outside?' Liam asked Carter, gesturing to the door.

'Nice meeting you,' Carter told Tina, he got up and left with Liam.

***

Carter and Liam stopped and got coffee on their way to the station. Carter had grown tired of the vending machine coffee in the office as his first fix of caffeine in the morning.

Glynn chased Carter down when they got into the office. She was another new face in the department since the start of this case. She was another detective transferred from another local department, like Liam. She had an English accent that set her voice apart in a crowd. Her hair was closer to white than blonde and was always tied back in a ponytail.

'Carter!' she shouted, as she came over to him.

'Hey,' he greeted softly, overwhelmed by her loud voice.

'Quick, you guys gotta see this. Popped up last night,' she said, as she began to lead them through the office.

'What is it?' Liam asked.

'It's our victim from last night,' Glynn replied. She led them to a small room at the back of the office. They all went over to her computer, where she opened a video.

'This has been circulating on social media since early this morning. Have a look,' she said, pressing play and stepping back for Carter and Liam to watch.

The video showed a woman crying, scrambling backwards on all fours from whoever was recording the video.

Carter turned to Glynn. 'Is that-?'

'Yeah. It's the woman we pulled from the lake. Now confirmed as our missing college woman, Felicity Madsen,' Glynn said.

Carter turned his attention back to the screen, where the camera began to shake, and the cries of Felicity got louder. It was happening in a run-down car park.

Felicity pleaded as the person recording the video went to the open boot of a car.

A hand reached out and moved around some of the things in the boot before gripping something and pulling it out. It was a machete. The screams of Felicity got louder when the camera panned around and began to approach her. The machete came down violently on her arm, which she had put up in defence. Her scream became high pitched as the machete drew up again, and she braced her bloodied arm with a large bleeding gash.

'Fuck that,' Liam said, turning away from the screen and walking off.

Carter endured the entire video and its gruesome outcome. There were five minutes of footage showing the death and dismemberment of Felicity Madsen. The face of the attacker never appeared on the video.

Carter turned to Glynn when the video ended.

'Sends shivers down your spine, doesn't it?' she asked.

'Have we found the source yet? Who made the upload?'

'It's been so widely shared it's hard to pinpoint the source, but our tech guys are working on it.'

'I think I know someone who might be able to speed things up.'

'Well, get them on it. We need all the help we can get. By the way, a search warrant has been issued for the owner of that lake hut, Jamie Penn. The guy you two were looking for. We're leaving soon. I can give you a heads up when we are heading out.'

'Appreciate it,' Carter said, walking to the door. He stopped in front of Liam, who was leaning against the wall. 'You okay? You look pale.'

'I'm fine, damn, that was fucked up. This guy deserves a bullet, not a cell.'

'I know. C'mon,' Carter said, leaving the office.

Liam followed Carter around the building. There was an increased sense of urgency within the building, with people rushing up and down the corridors and frantic shouting between colleagues in the smaller offices and staff rooms they passed. They finally arrived outside another office.

'Who's this?' Liam asked, as Carter knocked on the door.

Carter ignored Liam's question and entered soon after knocking. Sat behind a small desk and a computer was a mature woman with half-moon shaped glasses and skinny, narrow features. It was

Linda, Carter's former assistant during his time as a private investigator.

'Still no escaping you,' Linda said.

'I see you even tried switching offices, you sneaky bitch,' Carter said.

'Promotion,' Linda said proudly, winking at him.

'Who did you sleep with?' Carter asked, looking at her sideways.

'Fuck off, who's this?' Linda asked, pointing to Liam.

'New kid. Liam, this is Linda, Linda-Liam.'

'Nice to meet you, son,' Linda said. 'I thought you didn't want a partner?' she asked Carter.

'I didn't, but here we are.'

'Feel sorry for the kid.'

'Don't,' Carter said.

'Has he always been like this?' Liam asked Linda.

'You can't teach someone to be that much of an asshole,' Linda quipped.

'Need to cut this visit short because we're stretched for time,' Carter said.

'Aren't we all?' Linda asked, gesturing at the various folders on her desk.

'I need a favour. I need you to find the source behind whoever uploaded the killing of the Madsen girl.'

'That's a tall order. Have you not got your own people on it?'

'I need it quick.'

'You've still the same number, yeah?' Linda asked, just as Carter's phone started to ring.

'Yeah. Thanks for this, I owe you big.'

'Are you still going to the wedding?' Linda asked.

'Aw shit. Is it this month?'

'Really? You need to get your shit together,' Linda fumed. 'Of all the girls your friend had to pick, it had to be my niece.'

'Don't worry, I'll be there.'

'You better be.'

'Thanks for the help,' Carter said, before taking the call and leaving the office. 'Yeah?' Carter answered, with Liam closing the door to Linda's office upon leaving.

'We're heading out to the house, you both coming?' Glynn asked.

'On our way,' Carter hung up. He looked to Liam. 'It's time, let's go.'

***

Carter and Liam drove close to the small convoy of police cars to Jamie Penn's house. Some elderly neighbours had come out into their front gardens to see what all the commotion was about. Officers started to cordon off the street outside of Jamie's house. A small fleet of squad cars parked along the footpath, with a few others stopping any traffic from entering at either end with the siren lights flashing.

Carter and Liam joined up with Glynn at the front of the house.

Officers approached the door, announcing their arrival. 'Police! Open up!' They used a police battering ram to knock in the door and storm the house after no answer.

Carter could hear the officers storming throughout the house, shouting warnings to any occupants who might be inside.

The officers declared the house as clear.

Carter and Liam started searching the bottom floor with more reinforcements that had entered whilst Glynn disappeared upstairs.

The house had a stench. Clothes laid scattered carelessly around the house. A couple of cats scampered past their feet as they went to the kitchen. Carter assumed that the cats belonged to the household after spotting two feeding bowls on the floor next to the fridge. There were dishes piled high in the sink, and the kitchen floor was wet and sticky. The stench eventually hit Carter's nose, which forced him to hold his breath. It was a strong smell of urine, most likely from the cats. Liam went ahead and checked the back door. It was locked solid.

'Carter! Up here!' Glynn's voice called from upstairs.

Carter and Liam climbed the stairs and an officer directed them to go down the hall.

'In here!' Glynn's voice called.

They followed her voice which brought them into the bathroom where Glynn and an officer were stood while the thudding of boots indicated that the others were still searching through the house. Blood had stained and filled the crevices between the white tiled floor at their feet. Only one of the three spotlights overhead worked, making the room very dull compared to the rest of the house. Carter got closer to look at what Glynn had her eyes focused on. The bathtub was filled with blood, with splatters of it all over the wall beside it, almost reaching as high as the ceiling. The blood inside the bathtub sat undisturbed, with nothing rising above its surface.

'You checked it yet?' Carter asked Glynn and the officer.

Glynn looked at Carter with wide eyes and gently shook her head.

Carter approached the bathtub, leaning over it. 'Get someone in here.'

Liam went into the hall and began shouting out for a forensic officer.

A small team arrived after a few minutes and carefully examined the bathtub. Carter and the others watched on, waiting to find out what, if anything, the bathtub was hiding. There were not any other points of interest in the room. The sink was clean, with an assortment of used soap bars resting around its taps. A small cabinet above it revealed nothing but an old set of toothbrushes, and there were no clear indications of a struggle taking place in the room. One of the forensic officers reached inside the bathtub and carefully brought something to the surface, a human hand.

'Oh, fuck that!' Liam exclaimed, leaving the room.

Carter stood over it before looking to Glynn, who looked visibly shaken.

They all left the house after continuing and expanding their search beyond the bathroom. Carter, Liam and Glynn spent time interviewing neighbours, but they didn't manage to turn up any irregularities.

Carter met up with Glynn outside as she came out onto the street from another neighbour's house.

'Anything?' Carter asked.

'Nothing. No one has seen or heard from Mr Penn

for over a week.'

'Someone must have seen something, heard something at least.'

'Wait a sec, I have to take this,' Glynn said, as she took out her phone.

Glynn walked away to talk as Carter looked around the street. Liam approached from the far end of the street.

'Couldn't get anything from the neighbours,' Liam admitted.

'Yeah, same here.'

'So, what now?'

Glynn finished her call and walked back over to Carter and Liam.

'The team down at the lake found another body. They think it's Penn.'

'Has anyone managed to track the source of that video yet,' Liam asked.

'No word yet,' Glynn said.

'And the new missing woman? Anything?' Carter asked.

'Her name is Lisa Glass. It's thought she was taken from her home. I helped sweep her house when you guys were at the lake. Nothing untoward. She lived alone. Family and friends faced the usual questions. It's like she just vanished into thin air.'

'Any links to the previous victims?' Liam cut in.

'No, not right now.'

'Where is the house?' Carter asked.

Glynn gave the address to Carter and went back inside Jamie Penn's house. Carter asked Glynn to go with them, but she declared that she wanted to check over a few things at the scene. Carter took Liam back to the car.

'Why are we going? She said she already swept the house,' Liam said, as he climbed into the passenger seat.

'I'd rather check for myself to be sure.'

***

They drove to the house, which was in the seaside town of Bangor. The house was in a quiet residential area, just short of the town centre.

Carter and Liam saw a small crowd gathered on the road and footpath outside the house, still sealed off by police.

'Someone's tipped off the press,' Carter muttered, parking up a short distance away.

Carter and Liam fought their way through the crowd as some journalists were doing a live broadcast about the latest woman 'The Fisherman' was believed to have taken.

Carter and Liam showed the police officer guarding the property their ID cards and were granted entry to the house.

The interior was bright with brilliant white walls, glass-paned doors, crystal lampshades and a long hallway mirror. Combined, they all reflected the light entering the building.

'Hah, was thinking about getting one of these,' Liam said, pointing at the mirror.

Carter ignored him and started to look around.

He checked every room from top to bottom. The

house was spotless. There wasn't a thing out of place. Carter's phone started to ring when he was descending the stairs. He answered the call to an unknown number. 'Hello?'

'How are you enjoying it?' a voice asked.

'What?' Carter stopped at the foot of the stairs, halting Liam, who almost stumbled into the back of him.

'I asked if you're enjoying it?'

'That you, Platt?' Carter saw that Liam's eyes widened as he asked the question.

'Listen, how would you like me to save you a lot of time?'

'I'm guessing that doesn't have to do with handing yourself in?'

Platt sniggered. 'Afraid not. But I can tell you where she is. You'll not find her in that house.'

Carter turned to Liam and gestured to look around. Carter left the house through the front door and began checking up and down the street and searching through the faces in the crowd.

'Where is she?' Carter asked.

'Go down to the marina. On the longest pier, you'll find a fishing rod. I just cast it out, and I think I have a bite.'

'What do you want? What will it take to end this?'

'Like I told you before. You're going to make me famous, Carter.'

'How did you get my number?'

'A mutual friend. If you look hard enough, you'll figure it out. Wouldn't take a detective to solve that one.'

The line went dead.

Carter went back inside the house to fetch Liam. 'Hey, let's go,' Carter instructed.

'Where?' Liam asked.

'I'll explain on the way.'

***

Carter detailed the phone conversation to Liam on the way to Bangor's pier. Carter also made a call to get officers and forensics to meet them down there.

They left the car and began to walk out along the longest pier that stretched out into the Irish Sea. The howling winds battered the pier. People had begun to retreat as Carter and Liam advanced towards them. Carter saw a squared platform with metal railings that extended out. Rested against the rails, he could see the fishing rod. They got to it and saw that the rod had been taped and cable-tied to hold it in place.

Carter traced the fishing line down towards the water, but it didn't reach that far. Carter could see something on the end of the line, hanging just above the rocks below.

Liam's eyes followed Carter's, then he left his side and began climbing down to the rocks.

'Liam!' Carter protested, but he kept moving.

Carter watched as Liam clambered below the platform. Liam was right beneath him when he shouted, 'Fuck!' and fell on his backside.

'What is it?'

Liam took a moment to gather himself. He got back to his feet and looked up at Carter. 'It looks like somebody's heart.'

Carter looked to make sure no one was around. He went over to make sure that the rod was secure and wasn't at risk of being swept away by the winds.

'Who the fuck is that?' Liam asked.

'Who?' Carter asked, returning to where he could see Liam.

'There,' he said, pointing out a man on the other side of the pier. 'That asshole was taking photos of us.'

The man caught sight of them and began to run away.

Liam shrugged off his coat.

'What are you doing?'

'We need to get him,' Liam said, and then he jumped, landing with a loud splash in the water, swimming across to the other pier.

Carter started running along the pier to get to the other side. He dodged and weaved between the people on the seafront pathway. He passed the car park, the Victorian clock and the public toilets before he reached the other pier. Carter heard sirens approaching in the distance. They were finally responding to his call.

A soaked Liam came running towards him.

'Down there! Marina!' Liam said.

Carter diverted his path towards the boardwalk, his steps thundered on the wooden boards as he rushed down onto the walkway. Carter slowed, glancing around the empty walkway at the vacant boats floating silently on the water. The deck boards beneath his feet began to shake as Liam came to join him.

'You see him?' Liam asked.

'No.'

They both began to search each stretch of the walkway. Liam started to split off before Carter held out his hand to stop him. 'Where are you going?' Carter asked.

'Splitting up, we need to cover more ground.'

'Stick together. I don't wanna have to come and find you.'

They began to climb up onto the gangway so they could view the boats as they passed. A rumbling noise startled them, and they froze to listen. Another series of rumbles came from a boat up ahead. They advanced on a small white cabin cruiser with white sails flapping in the wind. The noises ahead had stopped, and the gentle rocking of the boats in the marina replaced them. They snuck up on the boat as quietly as they could.

A figure came into view on the deck. Liam sprinted past Carter and leapt onto the boat.

'No, wait!' Carter shouted, flat-footed, unable to catch Liam.

Liam disappeared over the rim as Carter rushed to catch up. Two gunshots blasted out, which made Carter stop and duck down. He kept his eyes fixed on the boat. It was almost within touching distance. Then there was silence.

Carter crept up to the boat when a figure rose above the edge, looking down at Carter. He had a worn fishing hat that helped contain his long hair. He'd also grown a messy beard.

'You've got slower, Carter,' Platt said.

'Bullets haven't,' Carter said, taking aim at him.

Platt hoisted an unconscious Liam into a seated position. 'The Chief strapping a new blood to you?' Platt asked, holding Liam so that he didn't fall.

'Let him go.'

Platt let go of Liam, stepped back and kicked him hard in the chest, sending Liam tumbling backwards off the boat and splashing into the water. Platt scrambled for the cabin. Carter hesitated. He looked to the ladder that led up onto the boat, then to the water.

The boat's engine started up, and pulled away just as Carter made his decision, holstered his gun, took off his jacket and dived into the water.

Carter had a hard time seeing below the surface as the water was so murky. He dived lower, reaching the rocky and weed-covered bottom and used his hands to feel around for anything that resembled a human figure. Carter quickened his search, knowing he couldn't stay down much longer without resurfacing for a breath. He swept his arms out until he brushed against something smooth. It was Liam's top. Carter manoeuvred to grip Liam and began to swim his way back to the surface.

He managed to get Liam to the pier and up the steps carved into the dock to get him out of the water, where he began CPR.

Within a minute or so Liam woke up and rolled onto his side, spitting water. Carter checked him for wounds, but there were none. He figured that the gunshots must've come from him.

Liam turned back to Carter, who rested back against the steps. 'Did we get him?' he asked, gasping for air.

CHAPTER SEVEN

Backup arrived at the marina but not as quick as the media. A journalist made a grisly discovery. It was the mutilated body to which the heart belonged. A cold caller gave the journalist the location.

It was the missing woman, Lisa Glass. Her body was within the confines of a children's playground in a park that faced the marina. It had been closed by the council for regeneration several years ago and left uncompleted. There was a large pool area with pedal boats in the shape of swans inside the park. They found the woman at the bottom of the pool with a large hole in her torso. To Carter, it seemed like Platt was bragging about his crimes now. Platt left the body in plain sight with no attempt to hide it. It seemed like a sign of overconfident mockery. Which meant he'd soon make a mistake.

Carter and Liam traded very few words on the way back to the car. Carter was infuriated with Liam rushing for Platt and being so reckless. Carter had recapped it for Liam on the steps of the pier after pulling him from the water. Their clothes were still damp, and Carter could feel the seat beneath him absorb the moisture from his trousers, despite his best efforts to dry them before sitting behind the wheel.

Liam gazed out of the passenger side window, which Carter was thankful for as he was in no mood for conversation.

It was late afternoon when they left Bangor. Carter stopped at a fish and chip shop, knowing they would miss dinner that night. Despite this, they maintained their silence to each other.

On their way to the station, which is where Carter had to go to speak to Paulson, a live broadcast from the scene came on over the radio. The discovery of the heart and the woman's body was now the main local news story.

***

Carter knocked on the door, with Liam at his side.

'Come in!' Chief Paulson's voice bellowed from inside his office.

They entered to find Paulson sitting behind his desk, one of his elbows resting on it with his head cradled in his hand.

Carter entered the room first, indicating for Liam to take one of the chairs in front of the desk as he took the other.

They sat in silence, waiting for Paulson to begin speaking. Eventually, Paulson leant back in his seat and locked eyes with Carter. 'What happened?' he asked. Then without waiting for a reply added, 'The crime scene manager told me about what was found. I mean, how did Platt get away?'

'He boarded a boat,' Carter replied. 'Then my hot-shot partner here decided to rush the boat and got himself into trouble. Platt incapacitated him and threw him overboard. Then I had to choose between pursuing Platt or rescuing my partner.'

'Is that true?' Paulson asked Liam.

'We needed to move fast. Platt was already on board the boat, and I made my call,' Liam explained in protest, firing a glare at Carter.

'Turns out it was the wrong fucking call, doesn't it? Seems you can't resist taking a dip in every crime scene. You training for a diving badge?'

Liam sprung out of his seat and began walking to the door.

'Where are you going?' Paulson asked.

Liam ignored the chief and left the room, slamming the door shut behind him.

'Have we found the boat yet?' Carter asked.

'I have our guys looking for it as well as the coastguard.'

'Let me know when you turn something up,' Carter said, rising out of his seat.

'Carter.'

'Yeah?'

'We're running out of time. We both know it's not a matter of if, but *when* another young woman goes missing. We have to find this bastard, fast.'

Carter couldn't quite find the right response, so he said nothing. He just stared back at Paulson with a look of mutual agreement.

Carter headed downstairs in search of Liam. He walked through the open plan office, but couldn't find his partner.

***

Carter swung by Liam's house to pick him up in the morning. He saw a distinctive green bike parked in the driveway with tools resting on the ground beside its front wheel. Someone was knelt next to it, stripping parts from its engine.

Carter got out of the car and walked over to the bike, where he found Liam's sister, Tina. Her jeans were covered in oil stains, and her blue T-shirt had been ripped in places, to reveal bare skin. She had her hair tied back in a ponytail which poked out the back of the baseball cap she was wearing. Carter also noticed – for the first time – that she had a neck tattoo, that looked like a rose.

'Didn't know you were handy with engines,' Carter said, announcing his arrival.

'Hey, yeah, well, I'm a bit of a dark horse,' Tina said, continuing to work on the bike.

'Is he here?'

'Liam? Yeah. He's in there. Hold this a second, would ya?' Tina asked him, dropping a ratchet into his hands and grabbing something from her pocket before taking it back from Carter. 'Thanks. Ya know, you should come round for dinner some time.'

The slam of a door drew Carter's attention. He looked up to see Liam exit the house. 'We going?' he asked bluntly.

'Carter's coming for dinner one night,' Tina said.

'What?' Liam asked, annoyed.

'I've decided,' Tina said, getting to her feet and wiping her hands down her jeans.

'Whatever, great. Let's go,' Liam said, going to the car.

'Thanks,' Carter told Tina before following Liam to the car.

***

Carter exchanged not a look nor a word with Liam throughout their journey. They were in each other's company, not by choice, but through duty.

Carter took them straight to the elevator when they entered the station. He pressed the button for the third floor.

'Where are we going?' Liam asked.

'Linda's found something worth checking out,' Carter replied.

They reached Linda's office, where she had already been expecting them, to interrupt her pacing the room. 'About time,' she said, going to her computer.

'Is anyone else in on this yet?' Carter asked.

'No, I wanted you to see this first,' she said, as Carter joined her in front of the computer monitor.

'What is it?' Liam asked with interest.

'That video of the girl being killed. I found the source of the upload.'

'Shit,' Liam muttered.

'Here it is,' Linda said after a few clicks of her

mouse. She stepped back for Carter to move in to watch the monitor.

Carter looked at the information on the screen. Below it was a map with a pin. The pin was within Belfast.

'Is this right?' Carter asked, surprised.

'I triple checked it. It's accurate.'

'Have you heard anything from her lately?'

'No, nothing since she went to Dublin.'

'Who are you two talking about?' Liam asked.

'C'mon. We're going to see an old friend of mine,' Carter said.

***

Carter and Liam drove over to the location pinned on the map within the university area of Belfast. They arrived at the building of a large newspaper corporation. Carter and Liam entered the reception through the sliding glass doors and walked over to a female receptionist behind a blue desk with the branded logo of the newspaper's name fronting it.

'Hello, how can I help you?'

'Is Ashley Kenneth here?' Carter asked.

'Seems word gets around fast, she only got back here a couple of days ago. I can let her know you're here if you want to take a seat and wait?' she suggested, picking up the phone in front of her. 'What's the name?'

'Joseph Carter. And thank you.'

Carter went over to a set of sofas, Liam, as always, tagging along behind him. They sat next to the large

67

windows that looked out at the car park, on opposite sofas, facing each other, with a glass coffee table separating them.

'So, you gonna tell me who she is?' Liam asked.

'An old friend. She's the one who helped me break the Pyro case to the public through the media.'

'I think I heard about her.'

It was the first time they had conversed since they'd been forced to enter the lift together, though Carter still would have preferred to have been there on his own.

He checked the large ticking clock above the receptionist's desk, constantly monitoring the progress of its hands. The phone on the desk began to ring. Carter tried to listen in, but only managed to grasp bits of the discussion. Then the receptionist stood up and ushered them over.

'Hey, Ashley said you can head on up. She's on the third floor. When you come out of the lift, turn right and follow the corridor right to the end. Swing left, and hers is the second office on the left. You will see her name badge on the door.'

'Thanks,' Carter said, following Liam this time, to Ashley's office. The building had changed since Carter had last been there. It had undergone a makeover. The door to Ashley's office was open.

'Carter? Get in here,' she called out from within the office.

Liam entered ahead of Carter. Ashley stood with her arms folded in the middle of the office, and she had an anxious look on her face.

'I didn't know you were back,' Carter said.

'Not many do. Who's the kid?'

'New partner. You know why I'm here?'

'Kinda obvious, isn't it? You traced the video.'

'So, you knew this was coming?'

'Yeah. Just hoped it was you they sent.'

'So, are you gonna tell me the story? The how and the why?'

'Maybe it's best if I just show you.'

She took out her phone, tapping and swiping at the screen before handing it to Carter. 'Press play,' she said, walking to her desk and sitting down.

Liam edged close to Carter as he pressed play on a video.

Ryan Platt was sitting in front of a webcam. Ashley's profile visible in one corner of the screen.

'Okay, so you wanted this interview. What do you want to say?'

Platt shuffled in his seat before uttering a word. 'I want to let the world know the artist behind the art.'

'You want to talk about what you do?'

'Isn't that what everyone is interested in? Including yourself?'

'Yes, you're right. I suppose everyone would like to know *the why*.'

'Why? Why not? I want to etch my name into history. History remembers the artists. It doesn't remember any other profession quite as well. It doesn't remember bankers, lawyers, civil servants or nurses. It remembers the artists.'

'So, you're doing this for fame?'

'I'm doing this for legacy. I want my name to be remembered. Even teenagers know who Jack the

Ripper was.'

'How do you decide who lives and who dies? Why women?'

'Because women are easier to control than men. Call me a coward or whatever, but it's true.'

'Are they random, or do you pick them?'

'Just random,' Platt said, shrugging his shoulders. 'It's simply a case of the wrong place at the wrong time.'

'Yesterday, the police dragged the pieces of a woman's body from a lake in County Down. That's a drastic change from when they were only drowned. Why did you do that?'

'Everyone needs a gimmick. Drowning didn't seem to be dramatic enough. The media didn't take enough notice. But chop a girl up into tiny pieces, and all of a sudden, they're in hysterics and The Fisherman is back on the front pages.'

'Do you think this is over yet?'

'Over? No. At this rate, I would just be forgotten by Christmas. No, I want people to be afraid to go out at night.'

'Everyone knows your name. Everyone knows who you are. Do you think that takes away some of the mystique?'

'It's not about who I am. It's about what I represent. As for the name, not my first choice, but I suppose I have no power in changing it now. It's gone international.'

'Is there anything else you want to say?'

'There is. I want to address someone directly. You all know him as the hot-shot detective. Joseph Carter.

Well, Carter. I told you that you would make me famous. Happy hunting. May the best man win.'

Platt's screen went black, and the video ended.

'How did you arrange that?' Carter asked.

'He reached out to me directly, through email. It's not hard to get. It's on the company website.'

'Do you know why he chose you?' Liam asked.

'He knows our history,' Ashley said, looking to Carter. 'He had terms ahead of agreeing to the interview.'

'Uploading the video was one?' Carter guessed.

'That was number one. He didn't want to be traced. He also wanted your phone number.'

'Mutual friend,' Carter muttered to himself.

'What?' Ashley asked.

'It doesn't matter. I need you to forward me that email and the number of the phone he called you on to find out from where he was communicating with you.'

'Done,' Ashley agreed without hesitation.

'And that can't go out. It's evidence,' Carter said.

'Fine by me.'

'You still have my number?'

'Yeah.'

'Good. Stay in contact and let me know if anything pops up.'

'Is that your way of asking for my help?'

Carter looked at Liam and then back to Ashley. 'Yeah, it is. We need all the help we can get.' Carter hated asking anyone for help. But although his trust was hard-earned, he knew he could trust Ashley.

'Okay. I'll keep you updated,' Ashley said.

Carter and Liam left the office and returned to the

lift, stopping off on the ground floor.

'You have a history with Ashley?' Liam asked.

'Well, you already know the details about the Pyro case.'

'No, I mean before that.'

'What do you mean?' Carter wondered if Liam knew more than he cared to admit.

'It's not hard to tell by the way you talk and look at each other.'

Carter had no idea that it was that obvious. He wasn't aware that they had looked at each other in any way that would signify it, but apparently, Liam had picked something up. 'It was a long time ago. Besides, it has nothing to do with the case, so can we leave it at that?'

Carter called Linda to update her when they reached the car park.

'Hey, it *was* her. She's sending across an email that came directly from Platt.'

'I've already got it,' Linda said.

'Can you see if you can get the IP address from it, and triangulate the phone number he called her on to get a location for him?'

'Already on it. Are you set for tomorrow?'

'Tomorrow?'

'It's Aaron and Pamela's wedding.'

'Yeah, I know,' Carter Lied. 'Thanks, Linda,' he said before he hung up.

CHAPTER EIGHT

Carter took the thirty-minute taxi ride from Belfast to the hotel for Aaron's wedding. The hotel was a stylish three-star that rested on the edge of the small town of Ballynahinch in County Down. It was a place that had always caught his eye from the road with its beautiful garden and trees on the grounds. He had always wondered what it would be like to visit.

Large trees towered over each side of the short, narrow road up to the building, which he found to be a little smaller than he had imagined. It was a two-story that overlooked a river.

There were people gathered outside the front doors in conversation. After leaving the car, Carter began to walk along the front of the hotel in the hopes of finding a familiar face.

On the corner closest to the car park, he found Linda. She was standing alone, smoking a cigarette. Carter walked over to greet her. 'I thought you quit.'

'I only smoke on special occasions.'

'Hey,' a voice greeted them both, from behind.

They both turned to Aaron, who wore a navy suit with a pink tie. He was well-built with a number three cut to his hair that grew shorter until it met his clean-shaven face.

'Hey mate, congrats,' Carter said, embracing him.

'Hi, Linda. Nice to see you,' Aaron said.

'Is it?' Linda asked sarcastically.

'You're looking well,' Aaron said, trying to maintain a smile.

Linda scoffed. 'You're still a bad liar.'

'Is this about what happened last month? I'm sorry. Can we please get past it? Just for today?' Aaron pleaded.

'Sure,' Linda said, stubbing out her cigarette and walking inside.

'Of all the women you had to marry, it had to be her niece,' Carter joked.

'Has she always been like that?' Aaron asked.

'You've no idea,' Carter smiled, patting Aaron on the shoulder and following him inside.

***

Carter sat with Linda for the short ceremony and dinner that followed. There were some familiar faces, but none that Carter wanted to speak to. He was enduring the day rather than enjoying it. His mind often drifted to the case. He kept checking his phone, that he'd put on silent, for messages and phone calls that never came.

Carter tried to relish in his daydreams as Linda got

lost in conversation with a few family members.

They finished the dinner, and the DJ got set up. The hotel staff moved tables to create more space next to the dancefloor, then watched Aaron and Pamela's first dance as husband and wife.

Pamela was short with brown hair. She was very slim with narrow features and didn't appear to enjoy the attention.

Carter spotted Ashley across the dancefloor. He stared a little too long as she caught his gaze and snapped his eyes back on Aaron and Pamela.

Once they'd finished swaying to the music, the dancefloor opened to a sea of people, who flooded onto it. Carter chose then to retreat to the bar.

'Two Jack and Cokes,' Aaron shouted to the barman, resting his elbows on the counter next to Carter.

'You got away quick,' Carter said.

'I'll get this round. My little brother stole my woman,' Aaron joked, pointing back towards the dancefloor.

Carter turned to see a six-year-old boy, wearing a waistcoated suit and bow tie, dancing with Pamela.

The barman returned with their drinks.

'C'mon,' Aaron urged, leaving the bar.

'Where to?' Carter asked, catching up.

'Outside. Can't go five minutes here without someone coming up to me. I just need a break,' Aaron admitted.

They left the hotel and went down a footpath next to the car park. It led to a sheltered bench overlooking a river below. They both sat on the bench and looked down at the water.

'So, how's it feel?' Carter asked.

'Strong on the throat,' Aaron joked, after taking a sip and choking slightly on it. 'It's good. I'm happy.'

'I'm happy for you.'

'What's going on with you? I haven't heard from you in months.'

'Ah, you know how it is.'

'Linda and I don't always see eye-to-eye, but she has talked about you. I think she is worried too. Said you don't trust anyone anymore, very guarded and live to work.'

'Well, trusting people and letting my guard down was what cost me last time around.'

Aaron looked off into the distance, as did Carter. Carter focused on a line of tall trees beyond the river, trying to guess their age to reach such heights.

'I saw Ashley here tonight,' Aaron said.

'Yeah, she just got back.'

'Have you talked to her yet?'

'I went to her office to talk to her about something related to my current investigation.'

'So, you guys didn't have time for a proper chat? A personal one, like?'

'No. There's nothing to talk about. She made the decision to leave.'

'Aw, c'mon. Are you guys not gonna try and pick up from where you left off? What about that conversation we had a couple of weeks after she left?'

'It was just how I felt at the time,' Carter admitted.

Aaron finished the last of his drink and stood up. 'I think you should both sit down and talk. That's my two cents. I've gotta get back. They'll be sending out a search party soon otherwise.'

'I'll see you in there.'

'See you inside,' Aaron said, leaving.

Carter remained on the bench after Aaron left. He finished his drink and enjoyed the silence. When returned, he found Linda still at the table with her preferred family members. Among them was her sister, Louise. She was similar in looks to Linda. Louise was pudgier and had short blonde hair, in contrast to Linda's dark locks.

Carter sat down again. He could tell that Linda had drunk a lot, and its effect was starting to show. Her face had turned red, and she was laughing at her own jokes. Carter finished his drink. He'd hoped getting tipsy might help him endure the night. He saw everyone in high spirits, smiling and stumbling into chairs on their way to the dancefloor.

Carter couldn't let his guard down no matter how hard he tried. His defences were always up. He thought to himself that these people knew nothing of the horrors happening around the country. Platt's next target could very well be any one of the women there celebrating with him. People generally thought that horror stories only happened to other people. Their murder a headline in the newspaper until it affects them.

He got another drink and returned to the table to find Linda in the middle of a story.

'Speak of the devil, and he shall appear!' she said, as he sat down. 'I'm just telling them about the time we were working in the private investigation's office. You remember the cheating husband you found who was out dogging?' Linda smiled.

'Yeah, but the couple weren't married,' Carter said, taking a sip of his drink, unable to find the humour in the story.

'Shh, don't spoil it,' Linda slurred, slumping over the table.

'Sorry, you go ahead. Don't let the truth get in the way of a good tale,' Carter said sarcastically, toasting her.

Linda chuckled and Louise joined in, followed by her friends and family either side of her. 'You believe the cheek of this fucker? I told you, I told you what he was like.'

Carter's attention fell on a woman who sat at the table directly behind Linda. A woman who was staring back at him. It was Ashley.

Linda noticed and turned to see what he was staring at. 'Ashley!' she shouted. 'I didn't know you were here! Why are you sitting on your own?'

'I'm not much of a dancer,' Ashley spoke softly, looking as timid as ever.

'Well, get over here, c'mon,' Linda said, standing up and making room at the table for her.

Ashley seemed reluctant to join the table, but Linda was insistent. Ashley wasn't the same loud, confident woman he remembered. In fact, she seemed a far cry from her usual self. He wondered what had happened to knock her down.

'You know who this is, ladies?' Linda asked, as Ashley took a seat at the table.

'Sorry, I don't think we've met,' Louise said.

'This is Ashley Kenneth,' Linda said proudly. 'This is

the woman who helped Carter bring down the Pyro killer.'

'Please, Linda. That's really kind, but it was all Carter,' Ashley said, looking at Carter but not being able to maintain eye contact.

'Nonsense!' Linda blasted.

'Linda, calm it down, yeah?' Carter urged. Linda's raised voice started to draw eyes from other tables.

Linda sneered at Carter. 'Can you at least admit she was a big help?'

'Yeah. She helped a lot.'

'That it?' Linda asked, taking another drink. 'She put her career on the line by getting that story out when you needed it.'

'Okay. She had my back when she was the only person left who I could trust at the time. If it wasn't for her breaking the story, things could've gone a little differently,' Carter admitted.

'That wasn't too hard now, was it?' Linda asked, spilling her drink. 'Oops!' she giggled, finding the spilt drink even funnier than any of her own jokes.

Louise and her friends hoisted Linda up out of her seat as a new song played from the speakers. 'C'mon Linda! We have to get up for this one!' she yelled over the music, dragging Linda off to the dance floor, leaving Carter and Ashley on their own.

Carter turned in his seat to face the dancefloor.

'Sorry, I didn't mean to cause that,' Ashley said.

'It's fine,' Carter said, keeping his eyes fixed ahead away from her.

He caught movement in his peripheral, followed by the screeching of a seat dragging along the wooden floor towards him. Carter turned his head to see Ashley pulling up a seat and sitting next to him.

'I should have told you I was coming back. I'm sorry I didn't. I just thought you might not have wanted to see me.'

'Well, you did find it quite easy to leave,' Carter said.

'I had to. I couldn't stay after what happened. I needed some time away.'

'So, what? Now you're back, you want everything to fall into its old place?'

'No. I just hoped you would be glad to see me again,' Ashley.

Carter sighed. Getting to the bottom of his glass, he felt awkward, with nothing to do and no idea what to say.

'Weddings are strange affairs, aren't they?' Ashley asked, looking around.

'Why is that?' Carter asked.

Ashley found a half-filled wine glass and drank the rest of it. 'Well, it's just a big party for everyone else at your expense, isn't it? The bride and groom spend thousands on the venue, the food and drink and the DJ. Among other things, of course. But at the end of it all, you've just signed a piece of paper after a ten-minute wedding ceremony then everyone gets pissed. I mean, why do people still see the point in it? I get the family aspect, but why not have a cheap wedding and an expensive honeymoon?'

'Each to their own, I suppose,' Carter said. He didn't think about it as much as Ashley.

'How would you do it?'

Carter looked around the room, studying every

aspect of the layout and the proceedings thus far. 'Well. Probably not like this. Maybe something along the lines of what you just said. Then again, not getting married would eliminate the numerous dilemmas most couples find themselves facing.'

'Still a commitment-phobe then?' Ashley smirked.

Before Carter could utter a reply, Linda and Louise appeared over them, dragging them to their feet.

'What are you doing?' he asked Linda.

Her face was so close to his that he could smell her boozy breath as she replied, 'You two aren't sitting here like loners!'

Between them Linda and Louise managed to drag Carter and Ashley past the tables and up to the dancefloor, just as a new song had started to play.

On passing one of the empty tables, Carter grabbed an unopened beer. He knew that he would need it.

Carter was stuck with Louise. He drank the beer in a desperate bid to withstand her terrible breath as she began panting heavily after only a minute. The women swapped partners for the second song, so he ended up with Linda. When the sixth track came on Linda pushed Carter into Ashley. They both stood facing each other with their hands by their sides until Linda came up behind Carter, grabbed his arms, raised them and wrapped them round Ashley's waist. 'Dance!'

Ashley held onto Carter's hips, and they started dancing awkwardly. 'Not how I imagined my night going,' she said sarcastically.

'You're as disappointed as I am,' Carter replied.

With their heads facing opposite directions neither could see the other smiling.

CHAPTER NINE

A bust manhole cover had flooded the roads Carter had to take to the station. The rain had been coming down hard since the early hours of the morning. The window wipers were working overtime to clear the windscreen of the spray kicking up from the cars in front.

Liam got a call and pulled his phone out in the passenger seat. 'Hello? Yeah, he's here. Hang on. I'll put you on loudspeaker,' Liam said. 'It's Glynn,' he told Carter before connecting the call to the car's Bluetooth speakers.

'Carter?' Glynn asked.

'Yeah, I'm here. What is it?'

'Where the hell are you two?'

'We're on our way.'

'Well, you're gonna wanna take a detour up north. We've got Platt!' Glynn said.

'What?' Carter asked in amazement.

'Our friends up in Enniskillen have found him.'

'Do they have him in custody?'

'They have him cornered. He took a tour guide hostage in the Marble Arch Caves after she recognized him from the news and raised the alarm. I'm already on my way there.'

Carter and Liam made the long journey to Enniskillen, a town in the northwest of the country. It was a favourite for holidaymakers and fishers. Carter's mind flooded with possibilities of what awaited them. Was it really Ryan? How could he be so careless?

Carter had only ever been to the caves once before. He had to use the satnav to find his way to the site. It was right next to the border of the Republic. The winding roads that swept the land gave the men a spectacular view as they travelled. There were hills of lush green fields, far-off lakes in the distance and the feeling of isolation and peace away from the rush and stress of city life.

They pulled into the car park fronting the visitor's centre to find it filled with police vehicles. Carter managed to find a space close to the entrance.

There was a buzz of panic as officers came and went. More police vehicles started to arrive. Officers escorted visitors out of the grounds, and water spilt into the car park from the surrounding fields that had flooded in the relentless rainfall.

They met Glynn at the doors of the entrance.

'Hey,' she greeted, as she entered the centre alongside Carter and Liam.

'What have we got?' Carter asked.

'One of the tour guides recognized Platt when he was here. She was the one who raised the alarm, but he grabbed her and took her hostage with a knife, going down into the caves.'

'Has anyone gone down yet?'

'Not yet. I told them to hold off until we got here. We're ready to move if you are?'

'Let's do it.'

They walked out to the back of the visitor's centre and into a woodland area where they followed a path that began to descend into a forest. Carter, Liam and Glynn came upon a large cave opening, hidden in the trees.

At its entrance, a small group of officers were waiting.

The men moved to the front.

'Okay, Carter and Liam you take the first team. The second team, you're with me,' Glynn said.

'We're splitting up?' Carter asked.

'There's a fork in the path down there. You go left, and we'll go right and meet up at the end.'

They began to enter the caves, and the first thing that Carter noticed was just how cold it was. They all walked down to a pair of boats waiting in a body of water illuminated by lights.

'First part is by boat,' Glynn explained, as she and her team boarded the first vessel, bobbing about on the water.

Carter and Liam took the boat behind hers, and they departed together, being steered by two guides. The boats sailed in silence over the water that looked like a sheet of glass. The rock formations on either side of the cave looked alien under the light. It was a unique sight. There was an eerie atmosphere. The cold damp air and silence gave their surroundings an almost supernatural quality.

They disembarked a few minutes later and started to tread along a footpath.

The caves were lit on the outside too, lighting the path and river below. The sound of rushing water echoed. Railings had been erected to stop people from stumbling into the water, and the walls dripped and the stone above them rained. Carter glanced down and noticed that the river was high and the current strong.

'Is it not going to burst through the rocks and drown us?' Liam asked.

'The tour guides told us there's a small risk of the caves flooding. So we should move along quick,' Glynn replied.

The caves had a distinctive smell, but Carter could not think of a comparison. And the deeper they journeyed, the louder the roaring water grew. Carter's hair had soaked flat, and water trickled down the back of his neck, past his collar by the time they reached the centre, where the paths crossed.

Carter and Liam led their group left, ascending steps that were slippery and difficult to climb.

The lights around them started to flicker, dropping the cave into complete darkness for seconds at a time. Some of Carter's group had brought torches. He borrowed one as he kept the lead.

Liam slipped on a wet rock, but Carter was quick to catch him before he fell.

A loud pop and a shot of sparks from overhead jolted them and made Carter flinch.

The water must have reached the wiring. They'd

soon be in complete darkness.

As they gathered themselves to continue the search, Carter heard distant screams, that sounded distinctly female, ahead of them. He began running over the wet path in a rush to reach the source.

'Carter!' Liam called out, but he kept going in spite of his warning, knowing they would soon catch up.

The woman's shrieks became louder, bouncing off the cave walls and over the sound of rushing water from beneath where he stood.

Carter rounded a corner and saw the woman up ahead. She was holding onto the handrail as a man tried to wrestle her off it.

'Platt!' Carter shouted.

A bearded Platt looked up to see Carter. He was wearing a blue baseball cap that helped contain his messy hair.

'Let me go!' begged the woman, fighting against Platt.

Platt did as she'd pleaded and ran.

Carter rushed up to meet the woman who threw her arms around Carter, sobbing. He could feel her shaking, she was sopping wet, and her long black hair stuck to the side of her face. Carter took off his coat and wrapped it around her.

Carter's group caught up with him, and he handed the woman over to one of the other officers.

'Take her back up,' Carter instructed, before running in the direction he'd seen Platt, with Liam close behind.

'Do you see him?' Liam asked.

'No.'

A couple of officers had joined their pursuit of Platt, but Carter and Liam kept such a pace, that the gap between them didn't close.

A loud rumbling started to bellow within the cave. The ground beneath Carter's feet began to shake, and stalactites fell from the ceiling, crashing and shattering on the path. Those that didn't looked like large glass spikes.

Parts of rock became dislodged from the ceiling and began falling in chunks, forcing Carter and the others to cover their heads with their arms and swerve to evade them as they sprinted onwards.

Carter realised the cave was collapsing under the weight of the water. 'Go back! Get out!' he shouted, turning and pushing the group back the way they'd come.

Glancing over his shoulder he watched a large part of the cave crumble down into the river, creating a loud *splash*. The wave it made started to chase them. So high it was that it spilt over onto the path, wetting their feet.

They returned to the boat, still docked beside the other, their guides waiting to row them back, but Glynn and her team were not there.

Carter stopped and looked back, as the others boarded one of the boats. He didn't want to leave her behind.

'Carter, c'mon!' Liam called. 'She'll be okay. There's another way out!'

Carter hesitated for a few more seconds, hoping to see Glynn emerge onto the path with her group so that they could all leave together, but she didn't show. Then, with much reluctance, he entered the boat, and they headed back towards the entrance of the cave. Rocks and stalactites continued to fall from above them, landing inside the boat. One of the officers got hit on the shoulder.

They got off the boat on the other side and dashed out of the cave, back into the daylight. The rain had grown heavier in the time that they'd been inside.

Carter looked over his shoulder, hoping to see the others not far behind, but they weren't there.

***

The visitor's centre handed out towels and spare clothes to those who needed them. The woman they'd managed to rescue shared emotional embraces with two other tour guides.

Paramedics and a fire crew descended on Carter's group, checking everyone for injuries and offering first aid to the officer who'd been struck with the rock. The fire crews were getting ready in the foyer to launch a rescue mission, but they advised Carter they wouldn't be able to go in until they'd been given the all-clear due to the risk of it collapsing.

Carter sat alone, dwelling on what fate Glynn and her group had faced. He started to wonder if they had made it out. It had been fifteen minutes since they had arrived back at the centre. Carter refused any offer of first aid from the paramedics and sat in his wet clothes on a bench. Liam had gone off to find a radiator to dry by. He was most concerned with the discomfort of his wet socks and boots.

Carter's eyes focused on the automatic doors that

led out to the caves.

'C'mon,' Carter muttered to himself. The longer time went on, the less chance there was of Glynn returning. A sense of guilt plagued him. Even though the situation was dire, he started to blame himself for not doing more, for not venturing back to try and look for her. No matter how irrational the idea might have sounded against logical thought.

He started to tap his feet on the ground in restlessness, unable to retract his eyes form the automatic doors, watching the trees in the distance through the glass, swaying against the gales. The murmuring of conversation and nearby footsteps on the hard floor of the foyer were drowned out by the thunderous rain beating the shell of the building.

Carter lowered his head and ruffled his hair, then straightened up to see Glynn entering the building with her group. They looked rather the worse for wear but were thankfully alive. And in her tight grasp, he could hardly believe it, was Ryan Platt, arms behind his back, face void of emotion.

'Take him in,' Glynn said to two officers that came to meet her. The officers took hold of Platt without a struggle. Platt smiled at Carter, but Carter didn't react. He watched Platt being escorted up the stairs towards the entrance.

'You all okay?' Carter asked.

Glynn looked at him, sweeping her long hair back with both hands. 'Yeah. We got out the far end when the place started coming down.'

'How'd you get him?'

'That guy over there.' Glynn pointed to an officer

removing his tactical gear while laughing at something one of the officers beside him had said. 'Roberts, been on the force for twenty years. You could say this is his biggest arrest to date. Caught our guy trying to jump down into the river.'

'Where is Platt being taken to?'

'The station at Enniskillen. Can I ride with you guys?'

'I need to find Liam first.'

***

Carter and Liam were allowed into the room beside the interview room. They stood watching the monitor which contained a live feed of the interview that was taking place next door.

Glynn entered the interview room and took a seat opposite Platt. He'd denied the offer of a solicitor.

'Where are the other girls?' Glynn asked.

Platt remained silent and stone-faced.

'Are they still alive?' she continued.

Platt turned his attention to the camera mounted on one corner of the ceiling and stared at it. 'Is he here? He is, isn't he?' Platt asked.

'Who?'

'Carter.'

'What's your interest in him?'

'I just wanted to thank him.'

Platt's attention diverted back to Glynn; his expression smug.

'For what?' she asked.

'For making me famous.'

'Is that what this is about? Fame?'

'History remembers the artists. Not the money in your bank, or how big your house is.'

Platt's voice was serious. Like he truly believed the words spilling out of his mouth.

'So, you think what you are doing is art?'

'Let me put it to you this way. How many people do you know who haven't heard of Ted Bundy? He's etched his name forever into history, just as we plan to.'

'We?' Glynn asked.

Carter stood and walked towards the camera.

'You didn't think just because you got me that this is over?' Platt asked. 'When it is all said and done, our bid to be held in the same esteem as our peers will be undeniable.'

'What about the girls? Their families?' Do you just not care?'

'It's true what I've heard said by some criminal profilers in the past. You do have to look at them as less than human. If you don't, that's when empathy creeps in. You need to stomp that out to do what I do. You have to ignore the tears, ignore their pleas. Once they're in my control, they're just body parts. They no longer have a name or meaning.'

'Sounds like there is conflict within you. Do you really want to kill them?'

'Sometimes you have to suffer for your art. That's what some say, isn't it? That art is pain?'

'Why is it so important to you?' Glynn asked.

Platt's eyes grew red, his voice went hoarse, and he sounded as if he was on the brink of tears. 'Most people live their lives in mediocrity. They work jobs that they hate until they drop with not much to show for it, most of the time. The only things they leave behind are children who may suffer the same fate, their dust and their debt.'

Glynn got up and signalled to Carter and Liam.

Carter and Liam entered the interview room, the creak of the door hinges breaking the uneasy silence just as Platt sat back down. Liam took a seat at the table, but Carter remained standing.

'I was wondering how long it would be until you got in,' Platt said to Carter.

'Sorry to keep you waiting.'

'It's not me you will need to apologize to,' Platt said.

'Is that right?' Liam asked.

'You two will need to play ball if you want to save any of them.'

Carter paced the room, keeping his gaze fixed on Platt. 'How many women are still out there?'

'Enough for you to keep on your best behaviour.'

'So, is this the part where I ask you what you want?'

'Usually works that way, doesn't it? It was kind of what I was hoping for,' Platt said.

'Then what is it?' Liam asked.

'No-nonsense with this one, eh? How are you two bonding?' Platt asked Carter.

'What. Do. You. Want?'

'I want you to help me publish my memoir. It's a kind of diary I've kept.'

'That'll never happen.'

'That's the price of knowledge,' Platt said.

'What about the families of those girls?' Liam

argued.

'I don't identify any of them by name. They never had names for me. Well, that's not true. Sometimes I made up my own,' Platt said with a smirk.

'We can't do that. Think of something else,' Carter said.

'That's the deal. It's non-negotiable, I'm afraid.'

Carter and Platt locked eyes for a moment. Neither one of them shifting, budging or backing down to the other.

Carter turned and left the room.

Liam and Glynn caught up with Carter in the corridor. He was stood leaning one arm against the wall.

'What now?' Liam asked.

'We call it a day. I'll speak to the chief in the morning. They will likely transfer Platt to Belfast then too.'

'You're not seriously giving any thought to Platt's demands, are you?' Glynn asked.

'Might have to keep the option on the table,' Carter said.

***

Carter and Liam drove back to Belfast together. The motorway was congested.

'So, are you coming back to my place for dinner? Tina won't stop asking about it.' Liam said.

'I said I would, so I wasn't being rude. But if you don't want me to, that's okay.'

'It's cool. We never have many people round,' Liam

said, watching the passing scenery through the passenger window. 'Just do me a favour.'

'What?'

'Don't try it on with her.'

They reached Liam's just before seven.

'By the way, whatever she has made for us, just tell her it's amazing, even if it's pure dirt,' Liam warned.

'Got it,' Carter said, getting out of the car.

They walked to the front door, which opened before they reached the porch. Tina stood in the doorway, holding the door open for them. Her clothes were a far cry from the tomboy look she'd had the other day. Her hair had been fixed nicely and she wore makeup too.

'Hey, how was your day?' she asked Liam.

'Is it ready?' he asked, entering the house.

'Hi, Tina,' Carter greeted her on his way in.

She closed the door behind them.

'Turkey roast. I hope you like it.'

They sat in the dining area. Carter gazed at the art scattered on the walls. They looked like original paintings. 'Where did you get those canvases?' he asked.

'Them? They're mine,' Tina said, adding salt to her plate.

'She did an art diploma, and now she covers the house in the shit,' Liam snarled.

Tina threw a teaspoon at Liam, which hit him on the forehead.

'What the fuck!' he snapped.

'It's not shit.'

'I think they're quite good,' Carter said, observing the one behind Liam.

'Liam's too ignorant to appreciate art.'

'Can't appreciate shit,' he muttered.

Tina raised her fork.

Liam saw her and offered up a hand in apology.

'How is it?' Tina asked.

'It's good, isn't it?' Liam asked Carter.

'Yep, great,' Carter replied. He decided not to complain about the overcooked meat.

'So how is Liam getting on?' Tina asked Carter.

'Not bad.'

'He's got a big fucking mouth, though, am I right?' Tina asked.

Carter almost choked on a mouthful of food as he laughed.

'Hey, is there any need?' Liam protested.

'What? You can be a mouthpiece,' Tina said.

'Really? You're going to talk about me like that in front of him?'

'What? Is he your boss or something?' she turned to Carter. 'Are you his boss?'

Carter felt awkward about the question and tried to answer it as delicately as he could. 'It's more of a kind of mentor role.'

'Good luck,' Tina said, pointing her knife in Liam's direction before returning to her dinner.

Carter felt the need to change the subject. He wanted to take the attention off Liam who was becoming annoyed at being the brunt of his sister's onslaught.

'That bike yours, Tina?' Carter asked.

'Yeah, had it for five years now.'

'You know a lot about bikes then?'

'I know a bit,' she said, smiling.

Liam got up from his seat.

'And where the fuck are you going? Is that all you're gonna eat?' Tina asked.

'Need to take a shit.'

'Such a gentleman,' Tina said, filling another glass of wine, then offered the bottle to Carter. 'Want some?' she asked.

'Can't. Driving.'

'One glass, c'mon. Give me that over,' Tina insisted.

Carter gave in, handing his empty glass over to Tina, who filled it up before handing it back.

He looked down at his plate and found he'd almost finished.

'Carter. Now that he is away. I need to ask you a favour.'

'Go ahead.'

'All the jokes aside, I do care for the little prick. Ever since our parents died, I've felt as his older sister that it's my responsibility to look after him. Try and look out for him out there, will you? It would mean a lot to me and give me some peace of mind knowing you have his back.'

'Of course.'

CHAPTER TEN

The next morning, Carter arrived in the office with Liam to a frantic Linda running towards them.

'Carter!'

'What is it? You okay?'

'I got it, c'mon,' Linda said, ushering them through to the office.

Carter followed without question. Liam stayed by his side. They entered Linda's office, then she closed the door behind them.

'What did you find?' Carter asked.

'This,' Linda said, pointing towards the computer on her desk as she hurried past him. She spun the monitor round to display an image of a marina.

'What's that?' Liam asked.

'That's where Platt sent the emails to Ashley from.'

'Where is it?' Carter asked.

'Carrickfergus.'

'Let's go,' Carter urged Liam.

***

Carrickfergus is a large town north of Belfast Lough. On a clear day, the large yellow cranes of Harland and Wolff shipyard where the Titanic was built are visible from the other side of the Lough.

Carter headed straight for the marina at the bottom of the town and pulled up in its car park.

A couple of police units were already out of their vehicles and swarming the harbourside.

Seagulls flocked above, swooping and diving. A couple of them were fighting over the scraps of food that seemed to have fallen from a nearby bin, blowing about the ground in the wind as the gulls gave chase.

The dark clouds overhead, were thick with the threat of further rain.

'Stay alert,' Carter said, leading the way.

They walked along the boardwalk, examining the docked boats. Some large, some small, some shiny, some consumed with algae, seagulls sat squawking on their roofs.

Armed police began boarding some of the ships and sailboats, searching them, and questioning the owners that were on board.

Carter stopped and surveyed the docking bay at the sound of something foreign amongst the whistling winds. It could have been a gull or a woman's cry.

'We could—'

'Shh!' Carter silenced him.

He heard it again, and judging by the jerk of Liam's head, he'd heard it too. It was a tired female scream.

Its source brought them alongside a white boat at

the end of the boardwalk. The dirt and decay more visible due to its colour.

Liam climbed aboard first with no hesitation. Carter followed right behind him.

They both walked over the deck, searching for the woman and anything that looked out of place.

The deck was empty, and all was quiet. Carter was first to enter the cabin.

The smell was the first thing to hit his senses: damp and rot.

The only light entering the cabin was through two small windows that barely illuminated the room.

Carter could hear weak whimpering from the back of the cabin. A click from behind startled him. He turned to find Liam's hand sliding down from a light switch immediately before an overhead bulb began to flicker on.

Then he saw the clothes covering the floor. And, the woman curled up, brown hair extending over her knees.

'Try not to touch or stand on anything,' Carter warned Liam.

This was now a crime scene.

Carter moved towards her, stepping over the piles of clothes in the gaps between them. Some, he could see, were torn, and others bloodstained.

'It's okay,' he said, gently, kneeling to face the woman, 'we're detectives, here to help you.'

On closer inspection, he could see the bruises on her face, fresh cuts and gashes. Saliva and mucus dripping from her nose and mouth, lips trembling, as she whined.

Liam called an ambulance while Carter remained by her side.

CHAPTER ELEVEN

Carter drove out to Maghaberry Prison. A high security prison a thirty-minute drive southwest of Belfast. He wanted to do this alone, so he had Liam go over some of their incoming reports in his absence.

Platt had openly admitted to the recent murders. Carter had more questions for him, and he was determined to get them.

He took a seat in an empty room to wait for one of the guards to bring Platt to him. It was a cold, cream room that contained only a few tables and chairs. The small, narrow-framed windows were barred.

There were echoes of slamming steel doors and footsteps. Then two guards entered the room, either side of Platt.

They left Carter and Platt alone in the room, closing the door behind them.

'I don't wanna play games today,' Carter said, as Platt sat down.

'You've got that serious face on. What happened?'

Platt asked. He'd groomed himself since they'd last met, his head clean-shaven and his beard a goatee.

'You don't know?'

'Know what?' Platt asked, shrugging.

'About the woman in the boat?'

'I don't know anything about a woman or a boat.'

'When was she taken?' Carter demanded to know.

'I don't know. I was in here,' Platt said.

'I said no games,' Carter raged.

Platt's smile and playful demeanour evaporated. 'Who else did you find on the boat?' he asked with a serious tone.

'Just a bunch of bloodied clothes. Why? Was there meant to be another?'

'It makes no difference. So, this woman. You got much out of her yet?'

'She's still in hospital, scared senseless because of what you did to her and how you carved her face,' Carter said.

'Well, that's *one* of my secret spots blown.'

'Who else is out there?'

'What about my deal? Have you had enough time to think about it?'

'How many women are still out there?' Carter repeated.

'Enough to make you seriously consider my proposal. It shouldn't be that hard. I'm sure your friend at the newspaper would be able to help you out.'

'And where is this memoir?'

Platt smiled and leaned in close. 'It's hidden inside a tree on the grounds of the Ormeau Park. Have you got a pen and paper?'

Carter retrieved his notepad from his inside pocket and handed it to Platt, along with a pen. Platt started to scribble down instructions, complete with illustrations.

'It's in a hollowed-out tree off the path. It is a V-shaped tree,' Platt said, handing the notepad and pen back to Carter.

'I can't help but think you're sending me on a goose chase.'

'Then I guess we have nothing left to talk about,' Platt said, rising out of his chair, maintaining eye contact with Carter before he walked to the door calling out for the guards to return and take him back to the cell he was staying in while on bail.

Carter got up and followed suit, asking to be escorted from the prison.

He took his time wandering back to the car, trying to gather his thoughts. He opened his notepad and looked at Platt's scrawled writing and scribbles. Maybe they were worth a punt.

***

Carter travelled back to Belfast and headed straight to Ormeau Park. He still questioned whether the memoir was real. Or if this was Platt's idea of a joke.

Was Platt having fun at his expense?

The park was busy as usual. There were people playing football on the large grass pitches and the footpaths were filled with joggers, dog walkers and cyclists.

Carter managed to get parked inside the grounds,

and he started walking up one of the paths towards the wooded area. He took out his notepad and began following the directions Platt had drawn up. The path took him up past the basketball courts and deep into a grove of trees. He spotted a bench, noted to be a landmark, and waited until he was alone before making a beeline for the trees.

He was not the first to venture into the forest, which seemed evident from the litter and empty alcohol bottles that he came across. He was now relying solely on Platt's notes and the hand-drawn map to lead him to the specific tree. The deeper he moved through the dense foliage, the less optimism he had about finding something there. But then he found it: the tree split into the shape of a V. Carter slid the notepad back into his pocket and ran over to it, in search of a hole where a book could be stashed. The base of the tree contained what could have been an animal's home.

Getting down on all fours he slowly reached inside and began scrabbling about with his hand, breaking spider's webs and brushing against small leaves that had blown inside. Then he felt something else. A smooth plastic-like rectangular object. Carter grabbed hold of it and dragged it out. It was a zip-lock bag, and inside was a notebook. Glancing around, he stuffed it inside his coat and made his way back to the car.

Sliding the notebook into the sleeve at the back of his seat, he drove away.

Thinking about the woman he'd found in the cabin of the boat, he drove over to Ulster Hospital, where she was recovering. But on the way he was side-tracked by a call on the radio; police indicated they had found another body. This time it was near the seaside town of Newcastle in County Down. It was around a forty-five-minute drive from where he now was. He knew the town well. He used to go there for day trips with his family when he was young. It was the closest beach, though he'd spent most of his time there in the amusement arcades.

The town hugged the coast of the Irish Sea. The beach beside the long promenade was one of the busiest in the country. You could always bet on it being full whenever there was a glimmer of sunshine on a weekend or bank holiday. People from all around would flock there.

The town sat at the foot of the Mourne Mountains. A popularised mountain range that offered breath-taking views and challenging hikes for those who wanted to brave their way to the summits. One of Carter's favourite childhood haunts was the trail that passed The Bloody Bridge. It sat on the fringe of the Mourne Mountains and used to be an old smuggler's route that followed a river. Carter used to climb on the rocks edging it, instead of using the path. But the constant fear was always with him, the fear of falling into one of the rock pools. He had a fear of water since he was young because he almost drowned in a local swimming pool while there with his school. On another occasion, at the Bloody Bridge, Carter slid on a rock, smashing his head against it before falling into a deep part of the river. He'd had to rely on his friend to fish him out. Carter could remember his great uncle telling him how the Bloody Bridge got its name. He told him that during the Irish rebellion in 1641, slain prisoners were thrown over the bridge into the river below, turning the river red with their blood.

The police had found the body at the Silent Valley Reservoir, nestled snugly within the Mourne Mountains. Carter left the town of Newcastle and began the journey up past the mountains to the reservoir, as the sun ducked in and out of the clouds, casting rays of light here and there over the landscape. It was quiet and peaceful, with just a few cottages and houses scattered around, until he reached a roadblock.

He stopped and lowered his window to speak to the officer who was heading towards him.

'Detective Joseph Carter,' he said, showing the officer his ID.

The officer studied it, then waved one of the other officers to back up his squad car, allowing him to drive through.

'Good luck up there,' the officer said, handing Carter back his photocard. 'It's disgusting.'

Carter followed the road until he saw the deep ridge cut into the earth. The pool of water glistening to his left, beyond a small stone wall. Beside which a building with a ramp where a small white tent, its fabric flapping in the wind, had been erected at its peak.

Carter parked his car, got out and started walking towards it, noticing that when he looked down into the water, was what appeared to be a large plug, like the one you might find on a smaller scale in a sink, just above the water level.

He spotted Glynn at the top of the ramp.

'It's grim,' Glynn warned.

'What is?' Carter asked.

'Another woman, maybe early twenties. A dog walker made the find. Looks like whoever killed her tried to dismember her.'

Carter looked down to where a forensic officer was working, made his way to the ramp and opened the flap of the tent to poke his head through.

A woman's body lay there, clothes torn, dress soaked, arm cut so deep it had almost been amputated. But her face . . .

Her jaw was missing, leaving her tongue lying loose over a flap of skin at her neck. It was hard for him to look, but he had to force himself to do so. The white of her cheekbone was visible through a gap in the flesh, and the only skin left on her face was on her forehead, at her hairline.

He left the tent and strode back up the ramp to where Glynn stood.

'Fucked up, isn't it?' Glynn asked.

'Whoever is helping Platt is just as sick as he is,' Carter admitted.

'It looks like they didn't manage to finish with her. I think they planned on cutting her up here, but they must've been spooked by something.'

Daylight had begun to fade by the time they'd concluded their investigation of the scene.

'Are you heading back to Belfast?' Glynn asked.

'Yeah. I might go to the hospital and try and speak to the woman from the boat.'

'Can I ride with you?'

'Yeah, c'mon.'

Carter and Glynn left Silent Valley and descended

the mountainous valley. They had only been driving a few minutes when smoke started to rise from the bonnet, forcing Carter to pull over.

They inspected the engine, but vehicular mechanics was beyond their skillsets, so Carter called for a recovery truck.

They escaped the cold by getting back inside the car to await its arrival.

'Always happens at the worst time,' Carter said.

'Is there ever a good time to break down?' Glynn asked.

'Suppose not,' he shrugged, looking out the window.

Then there was silence. It was an awkward silence as Carter did not know what to say to break it, and he had already guessed that Glynn was not the type for small talk.

'Did you always want this life?' she asked.

'Ever since I was a kid.'

One of his earliest memories was of play-acting detective, pretending to solve made up mysteries like an Irish Sherlock Holmes.

'What about you?' Carter asked.

'I come from a family of cops,' Glynn revealed. 'From my great grandfather on my mum's side and then my dad and my uncle too. Seemed like the course was already plotted out for me.'

'I had a hard time placing the accent, but is it Kent?'

Glynn smiled. 'Yeah, that's right. I suppose you're wondering how I ended up over here?'

'I didn't want to get too personal,' Carter admitted.

'It's fine. I was engaged. I moved here to be with him. I worked for the metropolitan police, but I managed to transfer, and I got a very good recommendation.'

'So, you're married?'

Glynn chortled. 'No, no, I'm not that miserable yet. My fiancé got cold feet and went running. I suppose I could've just gone back to England, but I was already settled here then, and I was just about getting on my feet, so I thought I'd stay and try to make something of myself.'

The recovery truck arrived an hour later. The driver returning the car to Belfast and delivering it to a garage before dropping them off to Ulster Hospital.

Glynn spotted Platt's memoir – which he'd retrieved from the car – in his hand.

'What's that?' Glynn asked.

'Evidence.'

They arrived on the ward to learn that the as yet unidentified woman had spent most of her time since her admission sleeping.

Carter entered the room with Glynn and saw the woman snoozing in bed. The wounds to her face had been tidied up and bandaged.

Carter walked around the edge of the bed as the woman's eyes flickered open.

'Hello, miss? Are you awake?'

She took a moment to take in her surroundings before focusing on Carter. 'You, you're one of the men from the boat,' she said.

'Yeah, Detective Carter. I was wondering if you wouldn't mind telling me how you got there?'

'I . . . uh, was taking a walk a few nights ago when I got into a fight with someone. They just came out of nowhere, like from a bush or something. I tried to fight them off, but they hit me on the head. They must've had something in their hands because I remember it was very hard and cold.'

'No one has managed to identify you yet.'

'Barker. Sonya Barker. I'm from the Holywood Road. My partner must be worried sick.'

'Then what happened?'

'I woke up and tried to get out, but the door was locked,' she said. Her eyes grew red and watery. 'The floor was . . . it was covered in these clothes. They were torn and bloodied. That night, they brought another woman to the boat. She was kicking and screaming. When they brought her in, she wouldn't stop. They didn't like that one bit. They began beating her right in front of me. I tried to help, and that's when I got these,' she said, pointing to the stitched scars on her face.

'Who were they? Was it a couple of people?' Carter asked.

'Just two from what I saw. After they were finished with me, they began ripping the clothes off the other woman. That's when they started taking the knife to her. I couldn't watch. I cowered in the corner with my head between my knees.'

'Did anything happen after that? Did you get a look at their faces?'

'No. They left with the woman when they were done and left me alone again. Then the following day, you turned up.'

'Are there any other details you can think of? Even if you don't think it useful it very well might be,' he probed.

'I'm sorry, there's really nothing I can think of right now,' Sonya said, voice breaking, tears welling in her eyes.

Carter thought it best to end the questioning. 'I'll make sure your partner is contacted and is told where you are,' Carter said, leaving the room with Glynn and the woman's partner's name and number.

***

Carter saw that there was a new car in his parking spot on his way to the main door of the police department. He guessed it must be his replacement.

Carter left Platt's memoir in his office before he found Liam in the kitchenette.

'Hey,' Carter greeted.

'Where did you go?'

'I'm just back from visiting the woman we found on the boat.'

'She awake?'

'Yep.'

'She have anything useful to divulge?'

'Not really,' Carter said, annoyed.

'Well, that's shit,' Liam said, leaning his back against the counter. 'I heard about the woman they found in Silent Valley. It sounded rough.'

'It was. I met Glynn there after visiting Platt.'

'Oh. How'd that go?'

'He isn't cooperating.'

'Did he offer to give up his partner in this?'

'No.'

'So, what's our next move?' Liam asked, finishing

the last dregs of his coffee and placing the cup in the sink.

Carter was hopeful that something would turn up, but he also knew that he couldn't afford to waste any time. He'd given serious thought to giving in to Platt's demand. He was sure there would be no issue in getting Platt's memoir published if he handed it over to Ashley, but he didn't want to give Platt the pleasure. And it wouldn't guarantee he'd give up his partner's name. He'd have to find something else to bargain with.

No sooner had he entered his office did the desk phone ring.

'Yeah?' Carter asked, running his hand over his head.

'Need you to step back out,' Paulson said. 'We've found something that's gonna blow this whole thing up.'

**

Carter drove with Liam beside him to a water park on the edge of Belfast. It was a well-known local attraction.

Carter could see the night sky filled with the flashing colours of rescue vehicles as the car climbed the hill out of Belfast before turning down a side road and passing through a police cordon.

They exited the car and entered the grounds of the park where they were met by a tense atmosphere. The place was a frenzy.

Making their way to an enormous, coloured,

inflatable slide that stood tall, like a sentry, Carter was almost knocked over by a police officer, before reaching a decked-out area at the water's edge.

Carter couldn't see beyond the crowd that had gathered but managed to spot Paulson in the distance.

'Wait here,' Carter told Liam, as he nudged and pushed his way to the chief.

'Chief,' Carter called out to him, once he'd got close enough to hear him.

Turning away from the group, Paulson walked towards Carter.

'What's going on?' Carter asked, looking around.

'Turned out there was another message your woman from the boat was carrying.'

'What?' Carter asked, confused, treading the gangway alongside Paulson.

'The doctors examining her spotted it on her back.'

'Spotted what?'

'A message.'

'Saying what?'

Temporarily blinded by the motion-activated floodlights that encircled the water park, it took Carter a moment and some blinking to unblur them. And when he did, he saw that Paulson was instructing an officer on where to go. He then gestured to Carter, with a tilt of his head, towards the water.

Carter stepped towards a group of people loitering on the decking, where he had to push them apart to create a gap.

Several items, tied to armbands, were floating on the surface of the water.

'Fuck!' an officer stood over his shoulder said.

Carter glanced back at him to find all the colour had drained from his moonlit face.

A human hand, discoloured, blemished purple and red.

There were a dozen armbands scattered around, if each of them held . . .

He shook the thought from his head.

'Carter,' Paulson said. 'I've never seen anything this bad.'

'Me neither.'

'I'm going to request that new measures are put in place from tomorrow. We need to close all public parks and attractions that house a large body of water. God knows where this is going to happen next.'

It was the first time Carter had seen Paulson's face etched in worry.

Liam approached Carter then Paulson continued.

'I need you to come down hard on Platt. This has to stop. We must do whatever it takes to prevent more women's lives being taken like this. We need to find out who else is in on this. Everyone is going to be coming for us now. I hope you know that. The higher-ups, the media, they're all going to be holding us to account for each loss of life since we brought Platt into custody, and reassurance that we're doing everything we can to keep the streets safe for the women in this part of the country. There's no wiggle room here.'

'I hear what you're saying.'

We're running out of time. Soon we'll lose public sympathy and with it, their trust.

CHAPTER TWELVE

Having questioned the staff that were at the park as well as the cleaner who'd raised the alarm and learning there were no cameras that could have captured the goings on, Carter entered the station just as Liam arrived.

Retrieving the memoir from inside his desk, he left the office, grabbing his coat on the way.

'Where are you going?' Liam asked.

'I'll be back soon,' he replied.

Carter got into his car and took out his phone to call Ashley. 'Where are you right now?' he said, as soon as she'd picked up.

'I'm down at Laganside Courts. Is this important? I'm about to go live,' she said.

'Yeah, it is. Can I come to meet you?'

Ashley sighed. 'If you can make it down here before I head on over to Bangor.'

'On my way.'

***

Upon his arrival, Ashley's crew were dismantling their equipment outside the court. Ashley held a coffee cup as he leant against the news van. Carter went over to her with Platt's memoir in his hand.

'Hey,' Carter greeted.

'This has to be quick, Carter. We are loading up to leave, and we are on a tight deadline.'

'It is,' Carter started, but then his phone rang. It was Glynn. 'Sorry. I need to take this,' Carter excused himself. 'Glynn, what is it?'

'Carter. It's Platt. He's dead.'

'What?'

'Someone in prison took him out with a shank. He bled out. There was no chance of saving him,' Glynn explained. 'Where are you?'

'I'm . . .' Carter started, looking back at Ashley. 'Nowhere. I was grabbing a coffee,' Carter lied.

'Well, I suggest we meet at the station as soon as you can.'

'Already leaving,' Carter said, hanging up.

'Carter?' Ashley called.

'Sorry. I've gotta go.'

Carter got back into the car and headed back to the station.

Back at the police department he learnt that one of Platt's victims was the niece of the inmate who'd stabbed him to death. The man confessed immediately.

'How could they not know? How could they let this happen?' Liam asked in frustration.

'An investigation by the Prisons and Probation

Ombudsman will be carried out,' Glynn insisted.

'There's mention of a girlfriend on the cross-force database but we don't have a name. But doing some digging on those who knew Platt I've been given twice the name Sonya Barker.'

'Sonya Barker?' Glynn asked.

'The woman in the hospital?' Carter added, grabbing his phone to dial through to the ward manager at the hospital.

'Detective Joseph Carter. Do we still have an officer posted outside Sonya Barker's room? Great. We're sending extra support. The patient is now considered a suspect, and we don't want her to go walkabout so please call the emergency services if she attempts to leave or shows any sign of aggression.'

He hung up and rang through to the control room for an emergency response unit to head straight over there, unhooked Glynn's coat from the rack next to the door and threw it to her. 'Let's go meet them there.'

***

There were squad cars parked in front of the entrance to the hospital when they arrived. A sergeant ran over to them just as Carter was closing the driver's door. 'Sonya's not here.'

'She's . . . gone? She can't just disappear. Who was stationed here?' Glynn raged.

'Toner. He's over there,' he pointed to an officer stood between two others.

'Toner!' Glynn yelled, storming up to him and slapping the packet of crisps out of his hand. 'What happened to Sonya Barker?'

'I'd been sat in that corridor outside of her room for four hours solid. I needed to take a piss. When I came back, she was gone. I was only away for two minutes. You should have had more than one of us watching her if she was a high priority. Unless you expect us to piss into buckets.'

'You request an officer swap with you, you don't leave a patient you're guarding unattended. She huffed and barged her way into the hospital, with Carter at her heel.

Now she wasn't there, there were two officers inside Sonya's room.

Carter didn't think she'd jumped out of the part-open window.

The CCTV footage they observed fifteen minutes later confirmed Glynn's suspicions. Sonya snuck out of her room a few seconds after Toner had crept away from the door.

***

Carter, Liam and Glynn spent the rest of the day canvassing the area around Sonya's last known address. She had no family, as far as they were aware, which wasn't a great help in tracking her down.

Carter knocked off duty when it began getting dark, letting the officers on the ground take over.

CHAPTER THIRTEEN

Glynn directed individual teams to carry out searches of Sonya's house, last known workplaces and other associated premises while Carter sat alone in his office writing out a report, admonishing himself for not considering their victim a suspect.

She'd been so convincing!

Linda knocked on his door. 'Where's Liam?' she asked, entering.

'He's off today. Funeral.'

'Well, I found something that might be useful. One of Sonya's old workplaces, it turns out, has been abandoned – for years. It's familiar to her, close to the main routes in and around the dump sites and—'

'And it's a long shot,' Carter interrupted.

'Will you just look at this?'

Carter sighed and took the piece of A4 paper, that contained a map, from her hand.

'The building was once an old animal testing laboratory.'

Which is where someone might learn to chop up body parts.

***

Carter drove down a narrow road, where grass sprouted through the tarmac and fridge-freezers had been abandoned in the fields lining the road.

A structure became visible up ahead. Carter thought it had to be the laboratory, but he'd expected it to be bigger. It was single storey that was falling apart.

Carter brought the car to a stop outside the large, rusty, graffitied steel gates. Feeling exposed, he cruised quietly round to the side of the derelict factory, parking it out of sight.

He crossed the grass to the wooden door that barely hung on by its singular, topmost hinge, and squeezed through the gap.

Treading on broken glass he could see huts at the far end of the yard due to the missing wall of the main building, and cages, that one might find in a kennel.

Entering an empty corridor through a snapped gutter, he allowed the daylight to guide him into what appeared to be the only room whose ceiling hadn't collapsed. There he found metal beds, operating tables, electrical equipment and empty trolleys.

Retracing his steps he came across a staircase, leading down, which he found, at the bottom, to be engulfed in darkness. Using the torch function on his phone, he illumined what looked to be a basement, the tapping of the soles of his shoes against the concrete the only sound.

He drew his gun, aiming it into the light as he descended, splashing into puddles of water, where he found litter floating on the flooded ground.

The layout was much the same as the upper level, though, despite the water, the equipment was intact.

Carter walked up the flooded corridor towards a set of double doors. He pressed against one of the doors and pushed it open and stepped out into a large circular room. An operating table had been set up in its centre, where on closer inspection, he found blood. There was a pile of bin bags in one concave part of the room where he found white tags labelling them: Site F, Site G, and Site L.

He dragged one from the pile, removed the tag and untied it, while keeping a hold of his gun. The wet bag slipped from his grasp, and something slumped onto the floor.

A severed foot.

A loud *crash* from somewhere in the corridor startled him, then the familiar sound of footsteps splashing down the stairs descending the stairs. He tried to hurry into a position that wouldn't immediately make his presence known, while switching off the torch function on his phone, but in his rush dropped his gun.

Wedging himself behind a medical cabinet and trying to slow his breathing just as a gruff male voice said, 'Well, he's dead now, so that's that.'

'I still don't know what he told them. That's what worries me,' a female voice replied.

Carter recognized Sonya's vocal notes immediately.

'Who do you want to put down next?' the man asked.

'The blonde, she'd be well placed at that spot. We'll come back for the others tonight,' Sonya said.

Sonya shone a torch over the bags beside a woolly hatted brute.

'Hey, look,' he said. 'One of the bags is missing its tag.'

'Probably rats scratching and clawing their way in. Place is rife with them. Just pick her up and get her out of here,' Sonya said.

Carter watched the man retie the bag and hoist it over his shoulder, before following Sonya out of the room.

He waited until he could hear their footsteps on the stairs before, hoping they were out of earshot as he headed back into the sliver of light, crossing the empty yard through the wooden door and then out past the steel gates. He crept round the wall to the side of the main building, back to his car, to the sound of an engine retreating up the lane.

Carter called Glynn on his way into the station to update her on his find.

'What has you so excited, Carter?'

'Belvoir Forest. That's where they're chopping the women up. There are three bin liners inside a condemned animal testing lab Linda discovered Sonya used to work at, containing body parts.'

'They?'

'Sonya arrived while I was there.'

'Why didn't you bring her in?'

'She wasn't alone.'

'So there was three of them, working together?'

'Looks like it. Unless there are more. They took one of the bags with them. I overheard them talking. They were discussing coming back tonight for the rest of the bags. They mentioned a blonde, so we can expect to find a blonde-haired female amongst the . . . dismembered parts.'

'Hurry back. I'll alert the boss. We'll have an arrest team ready for your instruction by the time you get here.'

CHAPTER FOURTEEN

It was getting dark when Carter parked his car on the street before the lane to the animal testing lab. Two other cars parked behind him on the kerb. They would wait there to block the lane to stop any escape once Sonya arrived. The rest of the team drove further down the road and used the car park of a country club before trekking up on foot. All the officers wore their tactical gear as well as face masks.

Carter and Glynn had worked together to sort out the logistics of the team during the stakeout. They directed their focus on the lane leading in, but they also had people surrounding the grounds of the laboratory. They were also under strict instructions from Paulson to ensure both culprits were brought in alive, which meant if they had to shoot at them they had to ensure they didn't hit anything vital.

Liam joined Carter and Glynn on their approach to the lab. Carter checked out his surroundings as they made their way up the lane in the dark, creeping quietly as they splintered off into their individually coordinated directions to their pre-arranged posts.

Glynn took Liam and went to where the large steel gates were. She found a spot amongst the shrubbery in the wasteland to lie in wait.

Carter headed over to the other end of the building, where the lane extended to the rear of the building before ending just past a large tree, taking up his position behind the hedge next to it.

Two hours passed. There was no sign of Sonya and the large man. Carter heard some of the officers becoming complacent and talking amongst themselves without trying to conceal their voices.

Carter scooted along the hedge to tell the officers to be quiet. There was a rustle in the bush next to him. He readied his gun and focused on the spot when someone popped through it. It was Glynn.

'What are you doing over here?' Carter asked.

'It's okay. My team are under strict instructions. They know what to do. Thought you could do with one more over here. You are undermanned on this side.'

The end of the lane began to light up. Carter and Glynn ducked down behind the hedge. The shifting chassis and hum of a large vehicle approached. Carter looked over the hedge and could see the dark figures of the other officers zeroing in on a box van that rolled to a stop just before the steel gates of the laboratory. It sat stationary with its headlights aimed at the gates.

'We can't let them get inside. Too many places to hide. My team are moving in now. I suggest you do the same.'

'Glynn,' Carter started, but she had already voiced

the command into her radio. 'Go,' Carter signalled to the two officers next to him before giving a hand signal to the others across the wasteland. Carter remained where he was, as still as a statue.

Glynn began to move, but she saw that Carter was not following.

'What is it? C'mon!'

'It's too easy,' Carter said, looking around.

'Whatever,' Glynn said. She moved through the hedge and slid down the small grass bank onto the lane.

Carter followed, sliding down into the lane. He stopped and turned to where the lane ended. At the edge of the building, he saw something move, someone watching. They made a run for the forest.

'Hey!' Carter shouted, giving chase.

'Carter!' Glynn shouted after him, but he kept his attention on the figure running for the trees.

He chased them into the treeline, weaving in and out of them and running over the forest floor full of leaves and fallen branches that snapped under his feet. He had a feeling it was Sonya. The figure seemed to be that of a woman, but his visibility was poor so he couldn't be sure.

Carter started to close in on them. He could see the spotlights on the football pitch up ahead, that shone into the trees.

'Sonya!' Carter shouted.

The woman stumbled, allowing Carter to catch up to her. He dropped his gun to tackle her to the ground before she could find her feet again. Rolling over on the forest floor, Carter managed to get on top of her. Then he felt himself being lifted and found he'd been thrown off her. When he got to his feet, he came face to face with the large man, who grabbed Carter by the throat, pushing him back against the trunk of a tree, pressing on his windpipe. Carter wrestled and clawed to break free from his grip, but the man was too strong.

'Let him go!' Glynn's voice called out.

The man took no heed of her warning, pressing harder on Carter's throat. A gunshot rang out, shaking the man, who loosened his grip.

Carter dropped to his knees, gasping for air and holding his throat.

'Freeze!' Glynn shouted.

Carter looked up to see the large man holding his side. It must've been where he'd taken the bullet. Then he spotted Glynn moving in on them, her steady hand focused on the man's chest.

'Don't move, you piece of shit.'

Carter tried to draw breath to warn Glynn, but he couldn't get it out. Sonya snuck up and smashed Glynn on the head with a rock that took both her hands to hold.

Glynn dropped the gun, falling to the ground. She moaned while trying to get back up.

'Stupid bitch,' Sonya mocked, dropping the heavy rock.

The large man went over to Glynn, lifted her gun, and threw it into the trees.

Carter struggled onto his knees before getting one foot under himself. He called out for Glynn.

Sonya and the man both moved towards him. The man drove his knee into Carter's face, sending him crashing backwards onto the ground, blood bursting from his nose.

A radio crackled.

'Football pitch,' Glynn uttered.

Carter rolled his head on the ground and looked over to see Glynn with a radio to her mouth.

Sonya snatched it out of her hands and stomped on it.

'Make this quick,' Sonya said to the man, before leaving through the trees.

The man went over to Glynn. He mounted himself on top of her and put his hands around her neck.

Glynn squirmed, kicked out, and she tried her best to throw him off balance.

Carter groaned and grimaced with pain as he began to fight his way back his feet. He had to help her. He managed to and ran towards the man, tackling him off Glynn. But the man unleashed a barrage of wild swinging punches at Carter, who threw his hand back, which the man caught, before twisting and bending it back causing Carter to cry out in pain. Using this to his advantage, he then lifted Carter, throwing him sideways against a tree.

The man towered over Carter, who was bloodied and bruised and trying in vain to find the strength to stand.

Behind the large man, Carter could see Glynn kneel and adjust her boot before rushing at the large man. She collided with the back of him, almost knocking him off balance. He grabbed a branch to prevent his fall, but it broke in his hands. Glynn let out a primitive yell and ran at him just as he spun round, the thick branch in his hand and it struck Glynn on the side of the head, sending her to the ground. He hit her again, harder this time at the exact moment the familiar sound of a bullet whistled through the trees.

The man cowered and stumbled, then began to run to where Sonya had disappeared, gunfire on his tail, denting the barks of the trees he darted between.

'You okay?' Liam asked, appearing beside him.

Carter ignored his question and dropped to take Glynn's pulse. 'Oh shit. No, no, no. Get medical aid here now!'

CHAPTER FIFTEEN

Carter was sent to hospital after the failed attempt to catch Sonya and her accomplice, who somehow managed to outsmart them. He suffered a broken arm, a couple of bruised ribs, and a deep laceration to his chest.

He stayed in the hospital overnight. While he was there, he heard that Glynn hadn't made it. As soon as he was discharged, Carter left for the station instead of returning home. His colleagues looked at him strangely as they greeted him. The cast on his arm was already annoying him. Even opening doors now required more effort. He also had to be careful not to bump his right shoulder on anything.

Collecting his replacement firearm on his way to his office, he caught sight of Linda.

'Carter?' Paulson's voice bellowed down the hall.

'Robert. What is it?'

'Can I have a word? Upstairs.'

'Sure,' Carter replied.

He followed his boss up to his office and took a seat in front of his desk.

'You should be at home,' Paulson said, walking round his desk to sit down.

'I know.'

'How you feeling?' Paulson asked.

'Like shit.'

'I just wanted to let you know that the body parts at the testing lab were recovered, and that of the woman you saw Sonya and the large man take from the lab was found last night on some wasteland outside Lisburn. But now, I really need you to bring this case to a close. We're losing trust, not just within our own ranks but from the public too.'

'The van,' Carter remembered. 'What was in the van?'

'A petrified young fella. It was a removal company. He was sent out there after a call from someone to lift building equipment. Sonya and her friend must have suspected something was up. Must have used the van to test the water. Hate to admit it, but she's smart.'

***

Carter arrived home. Struggling to remove his jacket one-armed, he was about to drop the blinds when someone began knocking on the door.

He peered between the slats to try and catch a glimpse of who was at his door but couldn't see from where he stood.

With his gun he walked towards the front door. Behind the frosted glass, he saw the figure of a man. He opened the door while pulling back the hammer on his gun.

'Took you long enough, old man,' Liam said, inviting himself inside. 'What's that? You gonna shoot me?' he joked, spotting the gun in Carter's hand.

'Don't tempt me,' Carter replied, closing the door.

Carter followed Liam, who walked on into the living room. 'To what do I owe the pleasure?' Carter asked, putting his gun away.

'I've got something for you.'

Carter saw Liam had something in his hand.

'I got bodycam footage from the forest,' Liam said, sitting on the sofa. 'Grab your laptop.'

Carter retrieved his laptop and sat next to Liam, who took out a wire and connected his bodycam to the laptop to play whatever it was that had been captured.

At the sight of Glynn, Carter suggested he skip it a bit.

'There,' Liam said, slowing the speed to play the footage frame by frame, then increasing the definition so the man's features would appear more detailed. 'We've got digital forensics working on identifying him.'

'Let's hope we get a hit. I won't be long here. I only came home to shower. I'll give you a call when I'm heading back out. Would save me money on a taxi,' Carter replied.

'Cool,' Liam said, getting up.

With renewed determination, he stood to see Liam out. If they were lucky, they would soon have a name to match to the man's face.

Leading Liam to the door and opening it, he was

met with by Ashley's smile. 'What are you doing here?' he asked.

'Wanted to know if we could talk for a minute. If you're not busy?' Ashley asked, looking past Carter to Liam edging around him, biting his lip, eyebrows raised.

'Come on in,' Carter said, escorting her into the living room where she took a seat on an armchair. 'Everything okay?' he asked, as she snooped.

'Yeah, fine,' Ashley said.

'So, what is it you want to talk about?' Somewhere deep down, he was hoping that she was there to speak on a personal level.

'Well, you know how I helped you out with that Platt interview? I was hoping you could return the favour. Give me something to write about, ya know?'

Carter scoffed. 'An inside scoop. That's what you came here for?'

'Carter—'

'You weren't exactly forthcoming about Platt, were you?' He snatched a photo frame from Ashley's hands and put it back on the bookcase.

'I was going to send it to you,' Ashley protested. 'I wanted to help you.'

'Why? You're not a cop. It's not your place to help me,' he said.

She gave him a disapproving look and folded her arms, then stomped over to the window, looking out onto the street. 'It was my excuse,' she said.

'What?'

'It was my excuse to talk to you, to see you again.'

'You don't need an excuse,' Carter said, wondering

how sincere she was being.

'After everything that happened? All the time that has passed? I think I do,' she said.

'Are you back for good this time?'

'I don't know yet,' she said, staring at him as if she was trying to decipher a puzzle in Carter's eyes. 'I gotta go.'

He followed her to the front door, where she stopped after opening it, turning back to him, so that there were just inches between them. Placing her hand on Carter's cheek, she tilted her head and kissed him on the other, casting her gaze down as though embarrassed afterwards.

He watched her walk away, his feelings for her reignited.

*****

'I got your message, Carter said, entering Linda's office with Liam, a couple of hours later. 'What did you find?'

'Do you not believe in knocking anymore?' Linda scolded.

Linda lifted a piece of paper and held it outstretched to Liam, who was closest to her. 'I think I've found your guy. It took me to a strange place when searching,' Linda admitted.

'Why is that?' Carter asked, taking it from Liam as he passed it over to him.

'After searching the criminal database, I took a look at civil service records. Just on the off chance, our guy was ex-military, because he does seem to be good on his feet.'

'And?' Carter asked, urging Linda to continue.

'Turns out, your guy works for the lifeboat service. His name's Ethan Conlin. He's been with them for over five years. Based out of Carrickfergus.'

'What's his address?' Liam asked.

'It's printed at the bottom of this,' Carter flicked the piece of paper. Then he turned to Linda and said, 'Thanks.'

'Let's see if we can catch him at home,' Liam said.

***

The road to Carrickfergus hugged the coast. The tide was out, exposing rocks and seaweed. A Castle sat at the edge of the coastal road, its large stone walls surrounding a keep at its centre.

The satnav directed them to climb away from the sea and incline towards the residential area.

They arrived outside Ethan's to where a small deployment of officers waited on the corner.

There was a car in the driveway that Carter inspected on the way to the house. There were boxes and empty shopping bags in the back seat.

'Police, open the door!' he said, giving it a good thump.

There was no answer.

Carter knocked the door even harder, 'Police!' he shouted.

Carter drew his gun, nodding to Liam for him to do the same, then led two officers round the back of the house, while the others covered the front and sides. They crossed a small empty garden to a wooden door easily booted in.

Liam took the lead upstairs while Carter swept the ground floor. No one had left since their arrival so if anyone had been there, they still were.

The house was empty too. The cupboards were bare, and the curtains were missing. Only their poles remained.

Leaving two officers at the house, the rest entered the prospective cars and headed to the lifeboat station.

The place looked old. Faded paintwork and boarded up windows.

A middle-aged man, plump and with an almost bald head, where thin white hair sprouted randomly sat behind a small desk. 'How can I help ye?' he asked.

'We'd like to speak with Ethan Conlin,' Carter said, producing his ID.

'Sorry, he ain't here.'

'Do you know where we could find him?' Carter asked, spotting a man stepping out of a door and heading into another.

'Your information is a bit outta date. He handed in his notice months ago.'

***

The call came in the following morning. Surveillance had a man resembling Ethan's description entering a new housing estate, still under construction, in Carrickfergus. He'd passed through a fenced off section of undeveloped land where a road curved around a green. They'd tailed him up a rocky street where a raised manhole skirted the pavement across from where he'd pulled into the driveway of a house at the bottom.

Carter arrived with Liam shortly after they'd received the call alerting them to the fact Ethan had thrown a jerry can filled with petrol at the two officers who he'd caught watching the house and had lit a cloth before threatening to blow them up and running into the woods.

'They must have some money to have afforded that place,' Liam said, passing the house and following the track that cut through the woods, which Ethan had driven through.

Carter relayed the location of their pursuit over the radio to Paulson, who was navigating officers to move in from where they'd been sent. With any luck they'd soon have Ethan cornered.

Liam sped up, swerving out onto the oncoming lane in a bid to overtake Ethan once they'd caught up to him, but Ethan was able to block off every one of Liam's advances, giving him no choice but to retreat.

'Any idea where he would be going?' Liam asked with frustration in his voice.

'Not out this way,' Carter admitted. 'Just don't lose him.'

The trees and hedges by the side of the road gave way to reveal the distant town of Whitehead. Ethan's car increased its speed as the road straightened out. To their left a service station became visible shortly before Ethan turned right, racing through the town centre towards the coast, narrowly avoiding smashing into a pedestrian and his dog, who'd stepped out in front of him to cross the road.

They swerved sharply along the country roads onto a narrow side street that rose to a summit of hedge-lined fields, where the trees ended to reveal a golf course, the blue of the ocean backing it.

Passing a cluster of houses packed tightly together, they came to meet the cliffs edging the water. Ahead of them, a tall white building came into view, Ethan's car parked out front. They followed him onto the grounds, where he'd abandoned his car, intending to lose them on foot.

Liam was faster and could make it round to the side of the building first, where they were met by a patch of grass fronting a lighthouse.

Carter tripped as a hand reached in front of him to grip his good arm, but he was quicker and used the cast to strike Ethan across the head, sending him stumbling backwards where he tackled him to the ground, screaming in pain, while Liam cuffed and cautioned him.

***

Liam dropped Carter off to the local hospital, where he spent several hours in the accident and emergency department getting his arm tended to again. He could memorize every crack in the walls and every defect in the seating area from the amount of time he had spent glued to his seat. Minutes had seemed to turn to hours, and every hour that passed felt like a day. They had had to recast his arm, and to ensure he didn't further injure it, put it in a sling. The doctor told him that if he continued to work, he could no longer pursue suspects, nor try to prevent them from evading justice with a whack from his bad arm. He apologised but didn't take heed of his advice. Instead, heading to the custody suite to interview Ethan, rather than go home and recuperate.

Ethan had been charged in the interim.

He was leaning against the back of his chair, arms folded, wearing a smile when Carter walked in.

'What will it take to make you talk?' he asked, without preamble.

'Maybe you could make my stay in prison comfortable. I want a room of my own in a normal cell. None of this high-security crap.'

'Nice try.'

'In that case, I'll settle for the list of items I'd like to receive.'

'Tell me what you want and I'll decide if any of the items are allowed on remand. And in return I want you to tell me how you met Sonya and Ryan and what your end game was.'

Ethan leant forwards, resting his elbows on the table.

CHAPTER SIXTEEN

'We shared a house while at university, in the Holylands area of Belfast. It also turned out that we were all studying the same subject, business.'

'Sonya was a firecracker. Loud and confident. Ryan was reserved until he had a drink. He may not have been as outspoken as Sonya, but he was no push-over.

'During our first summer break it was. Neither of us had travelled much. We toyed with the idea of visiting Australia, Indonesia, Thailand . . . but funds were tight, and Sonya wanted to go home, spend time with her family. So we headed down to the Ring of Kerry. It was Sonya's idea. It was on her bucket list.

'I was the only one at the time who owned a car or had a licence, so I drove. I had a part-time job in the off-licence on the Malone Road, which barely covered the cost of insurance and petrol, but it was okay.

'The journey to County Kerry took us just over five hours. We had a couple of pit stops along the way for fuel, to use the toilet and stretch our legs. Ryan and

Sonya both fell asleep for a while.

'The bungalow we were renting for the weekend was modern. It contained high-end furniture and a large-screen television It wasn't far from the town but was secluded enough that we wouldn't be disturbed. Without neighbours we could stay up late and party without worrying about the noise. We bought a pizza, which we ate as soon as we dropped out bags on the floor. Ryan claimed the largest bedroom for having arranged our stay. The other two were similarly sized, so Sonya and I didn't bother arguing over them. Then we headed out to the nearest town, Killorglin, in search of a bar. We walked so I could drink too.

'We stopped in a couple of pubs that turned out to be old men's bars, sipped a couple of pints then went on our way in search of someplace that had decent music, maybe a live band. That's when we came across the place where it all began.'

Ethan goes on to tell Carter about the sunken-eyed, straw-headed dude inside the outdated nightclub in the basement of a bar, where the floor was cracked, and drugs were being sold. Sonya, flirtatious caught the eye of the creep who followed them home.

'I fell asleep in an armchair next to the fireplace but was startled awake by a noise. I saw a figure sweep past the window. I went out to confront whoever it was while Sonya hid in the bathroom. The boundary of the bungalow was fenced off, there were only fields beyond. The sound of glass smashing forced me round the side of the house where I found Ryan already on him. The man from the nightclub. He had a knife. He plunged it into Ryan then had me by the throat.

Seconds later the handle of the blade was protruding from his back. Ryan didn't stop there though. He stabbed the guy over and again till he slumped onto the grass.

'Sonya ran from the house. I think she was in shock. Emotionless. She told us we had to get rid of the body. We erased every trace of our presence from the house, dug out the earth where he'd bled out, and stuffed his body into the boot of the car. Sonya found a place on Google Maps where we could dump his body. She reckoned salt water would make it more difficult to identify him. We found a long beach on the Ring of Kerry with a boathouse. We used a rowing boat to hoist him over the rim and into the sea. We checked the local news for weeks, but there was never any mention of the man. It seemed we'd got away with it.'

The second time it happened though was planned.

Three months after their weekend away Ryan fell for Taylor. A popular woman who was studying media at the same university as Ethan, Ryan, and Sonya. They met at a house party and soon became glued to one another. Which is why their break-up was a surprise. Ryan was heartbroken. He locked himself in his room and avoided his friends. Then the rumours spread on social media, claiming he'd given his ex-girlfriend a sexually transmitted infection. The backlash was insane. Students began threatening Ryan, he was attacked and so he started to isolate himself further, skipping tutorials. Then one night they got a call from Sonya, who'd gone out alone to a party back at halls.

'She was out of breath and hyped up. She told us to meet her at the hotel in Newcastle. We grabbed out coats and got in the car. We met her near the gates fronting the grounds where she told us to park and follow her to her room. The bed and floor were covered with tarpaulin and in the king-size lay Ryan's ex, rope tied and gagged. She retrieved a knife from her duffle bag and handed it to Ryan, reminding us of what we'd done, how the adrenalin had made us feel, how powerful taking that creep's life had left us. Of what Taylor had done to him, the hurtful lies and false accusations spread across campus. Taylor was thrashing and squirming as Ryan rounded the bed. He thrust it into her so violently that the bed shook. He drove it the blade into her long after she'd fallen limp. Then, rage quelled, he dropped the knife and slumped against the wall beneath the window, staring at his art.

Sonya suggested cutting Taylor up, to get her out of the hotel. We used the saws from her duffle bag. It went on late into the night. We wrapped each piece in bin bags and tape, changed our clothes, and took them out to the car inside the rucksacks Sonya had folded inside the duffle bag. Sonya directed us out of town to the coastal road heading south to a marina, where we drove to the end of the pier and threw the bags into the water.'

'How did Sonya lure Taylor to the hotel?'

'Well, she knew her, so it wasn't difficult to make some shit up about sympathising with her and pretending to dislike Ryan. Taylor was an influencer too, so Sonya said she'd help promote her social media channels.'

They had clearly defined motives for both murders, but the rest seemed to be driven by emotion rather than a lack of impulse control or revenge.

'Ryan got a rush out of it, he wanted to create a legacy. He knew we'd eventually get caught so he wanted notoriety when we did.'

'And what about you?'

Someone knocked on the door.

'Come in.'

The door swung open, and a frantic-looking Liam rushed inside. 'Carter,' he said, 'we've found another one. Victoria Park.'

CHAPTER SEVENTEEN

Victoria Park was situated next to the George Best City Airport. Carter knew it well. It was where he'd learnt to ride a bike. He even remembered the exact spot where he'd practised with the aid of his aunt. It was also a vantage point for watching the planes take off from the runway before passing over the park as they ascended the sky. The park had undergone a facelift, since he'd been a kid. New pathways had been constructed and lighting had been added to them. Belfast Lough ran into the lake that encircled an island containing a football field. The park was known for its birdlife. It was home to swans, ducks, and herons.

Liam walked alongside him through the park, entering a small tunnel underneath the carriageway, where the rumbling cars above them vibrated down through the concrete walls and echoed out onto the park. Black railings lined the shallow lake, where a crowd of officers had cordoned off the scene.

The dog walker with the Alsatian who'd discovered

the bloated corpse stood beside them. Liam stopped and stayed to take his statement.

Flashing his ID at the officer Carter bent under the police tape and descended the tiled bank. His view of her face was obstructed by the hull of the boat. She lay on her side, clothes torn and slashed. He rounded the boat, expression falling when he saw her familiar face.

Gagging, he made it back up the bank, and catching sight of his features, Liam raced down past him, ignoring his command not to. He dropped to his knees and wailed as tears fell down his face.

'Tina!'

CHAPTER EIGHTEEN

Carter took a taxi to the station. His phone rang just as he arrived.

'I got a lift into the station from someone on night shift. I'm sorry I just realised I hadn't told you,' Liam said.

'It's alright. I'm in a taxi. I'll be with you soon.'

He couldn't fault Liam for forgetting.

He directed the driver to the department, where he found a dejected-looking Liam leaving Paulson's office.

'Liam?' he said, noting his downcast eyes and shuffling feet.

'I'm out.'

'What?'

'I'm off the case.'

'Let me have a word with the boss.'

'There's no point,' Liam replied, stepping out in front of him

But Liam side-stepped him, heading for the stairs.

'Wait downstairs for me,' he called after him, before

shoving open the door to Paulson's office and striding up to his desk.

He fired an aggressive look at Carter then, aiming his words down the line of the phone he held in his hand said, 'I'll have to call you back, sorry. Ten minutes.' Then to Carter he started, 'What the—'

'Why did you remove Liam from the investigation?' he interrupted.

'Is it not obvious?' Paulson snapped. 'Besides, I'd have thought you'd be only too happy to get rid of him. Or have you warmed to him? Anyway, the rules dictate he can't operate an investigation with a personal link to the case, so he had to go. The choice was out of my hands, Joseph.'

Carter stormed from the room and slammed the door shut behind him.

He walked down the corridor, stopping halfway to punch it, before leaning his forehead against it and exhaling his frustration. By the time he reached the open-plan office downstairs, he had calmed down.

He found Liam talking to Linda.

'C'mon,' he urged Liam.

'Where?' Liam asked.

'You need a place to stay, don't ya? You can't go back to the house, it's a crime scene. And you can't afford a hotel for the fourth night in a row now that you're out of a job.'

Liam caught up to him as he left the building.

'You got any clothes?' Carter asked, as they entered the car park.

'Only what I'm wearing.'

'I'm bound to have a few things that fit you,' he said,

as they reached his car, which hadn't been driven since Liam had been recovering from the sudden loss of his sister.

'*Your* things?'

'Yeah. You can stay at my place,' Carter said, throwing the key to Liam.

He didn't protest and remained silent throughout their journey.

Carter handed Liam a change of clothes and showed him into the spare bedroom. 'I've got to go back to the station. I'm technically on shift.'

'Right?' Liam mumbled.

'You going to be okay?'

'Yeah.

Desmond, one of the detectives working from the unit gave Carter a ride over to Liam's house.

He felt like an intruder. This was his colleague's house. A man he now considered a friend.

The handle on the back door was broken, and the frame was damaged where it had been forced open. There was no sign of a struggle, which meant if Tina had been taken from here, she hadn't put up much of a struggle. With nothing to go on, Carter ordered a taxi to Ashley's, rather than calling Desmond for another lift. He knocked with his unique rat-a-tat-tat, but she didn't answer the door. Though he knew she was in as her car was parked outside. He stepped back from the porch to glance through the windows that weren't curtained and rang her. Positive he heard the notes of a mobile phone chiming from inside the house he climbed the gate at the side of the building.

'Ashley!' he shouted, but there was no reply.

His phone rang.

He answered it when he saw that kit was Ashley but didn't allow his shoulders to drop until he heard her voice.

'What do you want?'

'Where are you?' he asked.

'At work. Why?'

Carter breathed a sigh of relief. 'I'm at your house. I came to talk to you, but there was no answer and . . . I'm sorry it's just that with what happened to Tina I panicked and thought . . . I'm sorry. I'm just on-edge.'

'I understand. Maybe we can meet up tomorrow night?'

'Sounds good. I'll speak to you then.'

***

Carter returned home to find Liam slouched on the sofa watching football in the living room.

'I see you've made yourself at home.'

'Mi casa, es su casa,' Liam replied, with a mouthful of crisps.

He smirked and headed to the kitchen to make coffee.

Liam was putting on a brave face.

'Who's playing?' Carter asked, joining him, cup of steaming caffeine in hand a couple of minutes later.

'Liverpool versus Chelsea.'

'Who's your team?'

'Chelsea.'

'Ah.'

'I suppose that makes you a Liverpool fan?'

'Sure does.'

Both invested in the game, yelling positive affirmations at the players, the first half ended with Chelsea scoring right before Liverpool equalised it, prompting Carter to celebrate and taunt Liam.

The match seemed to have helped them both forget about the things that had gone on outside of that room. When it ended, Carter tried to find something else to hold their attention.

'Never knew you were the jewellery type,' Liam said, pointing at Carter's hand.

Carter had been toying with the ring that hung from a thin black leather necklace around his neck, out of habit.

'It's not mine.'

'Whose is it then?'

Carter hesitated for a moment before he replied. 'Emily's.'

Liam bit his lower lip and nodded. He knew the story. Everyone at the department did. It had belonged to Carter's niece, who'd become a victim of the last killer he'd crossed paths with.

'Tina was all I had,' Liam admitted. 'After our parents died, she was the one who kept us afloat. Seemed like after they died, she was the only person I felt I could relate to.'

'My parents weren't around to bring me up either,' Carter admitted. 'After my mum died, I felt like my dad lacked interest in me. I think he was glad to wash his hands of me to be honest. My Aunt took me in. She was the one who raised me.'

'Never stop thanking her. People don't know a good

thing until it's gone.'

Carter paused before responding. 'She, uh . . . passed away a few years ago.'

'Sorry.'

'It's always the good ones that go first.'

'I wanted to let you know that they're letting me back into the house tomorrow morning.'

'Oh, that's good.'

'Yeah, so just wanted to say thanks and all that, for letting me stay. I know you're leaving early in the morning, so I probably won't see you once I've gone to bed. But will you let me know when you've found her. Sonya. And what happens to her and Ethan.'

'Of course.'

CHAPTER NINETEEN

The closer Liam got to the house, the greater his anxiety. He had always returned home to find Tina tending to something, quick to poke fun at him over whatever came to mind first, rearranging furniture or working on her bike. But Liam was coming back to a house filled only with memories.

He reached the front gate, inhaled a long steady breath before opening it and exhaled slowly as he trod the path to the front door.

The place was spotless. The investigators had done a good job of tidying up after themselves, or perhaps there had been nothing at all to tidy. He ran his hand along the kitchen countertop then paced the living room. It was a while before he could garner the courage to journey upstairs.

The second door on the right at the end of the hall was Tina's room. He moved towards it, longing to hear her call out from behind the door.

She may have been a bit of a tomboy, but her room

burst with shades of pink. There were teddy bears on her bed, posters of singers covered her walls, and a large-screen TV sat on a unit facing her queen-size bed. It was reminiscent of a teenager's bedroom, but that was her; multi-layered.

Liam lowered himself onto her bed, causing one of the bears to topple over onto him. He lifted it to replace it then hesitated, remembering that one. He had given it to her as a birthday present, He was about fifteen, so it must have been the year after their parents had died.

It had fallen to him to break the news to his younger sister. A neighbour was babysitting them that night. The night of the accident. They had no extended family. Their father was an orphan. Their mother had fled her native home of Scotland to escape her toxic parents.

Tina got a job at the local supermarket to support herself and Liam. Their parents' life insurance policies paid off the remainder of the mortgage on the house, but Tina needed her job to put food on the table. She encouraged Liam to stay in school, taking on the burden of financing the bills, becoming both big sister and mum, while he became a recluse.

He had some friends, but he was always the joker, straying from the deep conversations or any expression of emotion. Tina was the only person he felt able to confide in. She was the only other person in the world that he felt could understand him, relate to him. None of his girlfriends could get through to him, but it was not due to their lack of trying. His friendships began to dwindle as the years extended until he reached university.

Most of his friends had moved to England to study

while Liam stayed in Northern Ireland. Over time, they all drifted apart, and Liam lost himself to his career.

He put the bear back and got up, straightened the duvet and took one more look around, before leaving the room.

CHAPTER TWENTY

There was an unusual atmosphere in the station when Carter arrived the following day. Eyes traced him through the building to his office. As he reached the door a detective warned him the boss wanted a word.

He was expecting a dressing down.

'In,' Paulson bellowed, after he'd knocked.

'What's that?'

Paulson ran the paused footage for him to see. On the screen of his computer was Ashley, bound to a chair. She spoke as though reading from a script.

'This is a message for Detective Joseph Carter. I am being held by The Fisherman. On behalf of my captors, it has become apparent that the time has come to disappear. But before they do, they have one more life left to take. It is up to Detective Carter whose life that will be. If Carter does not give himself up, I will become the last victim in his place. We will be in touch. And don't bother trying to trace the video this time,' Ashley finished, looking at the camera with tears running down her face.

The video cut to black.

Carter's stomach sank.

'Sonya must've known about your connection to Ashley,' the Chief said.

'When was this posted?' Carter asked.

'This morning. When was the last time you had contact with Ashley?'

'I . . . I'm not sure.'

'I'm having a couple of officers keep watch over you. We may not always see eye to eye, but I know that noble side of you. I can't have you giving in to their demands. I also want you to notify us if Ashley or Sonya get in touch with you.'

'Yes, sure.'

Carter had not felt this helpless in a while.

He entered Linda's office, forgetting to knock in his rush.

'Did they find anything at Ethan's house?' Carter asked.

'If there was, it was burnt to a crisp. The fire crews managed to put the fire out before it took out the bottom floor, but upstairs was ruined.'

Just then his phone rang. He pulled it out of his vest.

'It's Ashley,' he whispered to Linda before answering.

She indicated that she was going to get someone from digital forensics to trace the call by triangulating the signal, which in all likelihood would be once Ashley had hung up.

'Hello?'

'You alone?' Sonya asked.

'Yeah,' he lied.

'It's time. I suspect you're going to do the noble thing here?' Sonya asked.

'Where are you?' he asked.

'Lisnasharragh Leisure Centre. Don't keep us waiting.

Sonya cut the call.

***

Carter left the taxi, thanking the driver for losing the two police officers who'd followed them from the station to the junction before the leisure centre, where he'd managed to cut them off, manoeuvring swiftly left while ahead of them they continued straight on.

He followed the footpath to the locked gates.

To the side of the building was an open door.

The corridor was lit only by the green light of the emergency sign above the fire exit. The large glass windows enabled the fading sunlight to bounce off the polished floor. The place smelt strongly of disinfectant. He'd never been here before, so this was unchartered territory. He had no idea where to go so followed the corridor down and around past empty function rooms, and the half-plastic-sheet-covered swimming pool.

He opened the glass-fronted double doors, footsteps echoing off the stone skirting the pool and walked towards the three-tier diving board, half-expecting someone to jump out from between the quickly darkening spectator's seats that faced them.

'Carter,' a familiar voice sang from somewhere nearby.

'Let her go!' Carter commanded, as Sonya stepped out of the darkness, holding onto a struggling Ashley, who'd been gagged and bound by the wrists.

'You know what to do. Your life for hers.'

'The water was deep. He stepped away from the edge.

'Okay,' he said, palms up in surrender.

What he really wanted to know was why, but those questions he could ask her later. Once she was behind bars.

He noticed then how Ashley stood: awkwardly. He tore his eyes away from her desperately pleading face to her ankles and the object that had been tied around them.

Oh no. She was intending to drown her, alive.

'Here you go then,' Sonya said. 'Take her.' Then she shoved Ashley into the water. But weighted down as she was, she spun as she fell, feet first, into the water, disappearing below the surface with a *splash*.

Carter rushed towards the water, but one-armed he was unable to swim. He dropped into the pool anyway. He was her only chance of survival.

CHAPTER TWENTY-ONE

The water shot up his nose and rushed into his ears.

Carter descended to the bottom of the pool, chest tight, muscles aching from lack of use. He hadn't swum in a long while. He swung his one usable hand out to catch a hold of Ashley and caught one of her arms as she flailed in panic, to let her know he was there with her. He lowered himself to her feet and began to untie the rope that bound the weights to her ankles, as his energy began to diminish, limbs sluggish, coordination compromised, weakened from lack of oxygen.

He didn't have long.

There was a disturbance in the water then, a rush of movement brushed past him. Someone grabbed him round the chest and dragged him back to the surface.

He inhaled a lungful of air as soon as he broke the barrier and clung to the edge of the pool. His rescuer had dived back in.

CHAPTER TWENTY-TWO

Liam hadn't been able to relax. He and Carter had made a good team. At least he thought so anyway. They'd been through a few scrapes together and now Carter was facing them alone.

Liam had gone to the station and caught Linda exiting the building, who had informed him that Carter had left in a taxi without telling anyone where he was going. That two police officers following the taxi had lost him. And that the taxi company had told her when she called that he'd been dropped off at the leisure centre.

So there he was, coughing and spluttering as he emerged from the chlorinated water to lay Ashley upon the poolside. He ripped the tape from her mouth before pumping the water she'd swallowed from her stomach with a few chest compressions until she gasped for air.

He rolled her onto her side then left Carter to tend to her while he went in search of Sonya.

Liam sprinted towards the nearest exit with haste, bursting out of the fire door that led into the car park, causing the alarm to sound. The security company would be here soon. Help was on its way.

He heard a screech of tyres and saw the glint of the car's rear lights flicker as the vehicle swung out onto the road.

He mounted the bike he'd come here on – Tina's – pulled on his helmet and sped after the woman whose image he'd caught in the driver's window: Sonya.

He revved the engine and put his foot down, overtaking cars to skip the traffic. Leaning so hard to turn at one point he almost grazed his knee against the tarmac.

Sonya drove erratically, entering the wrong lane several times to outrun him. But she wasn't used to high-speed chases.

The vibration of the engine rippled up from his legs to his torso. He felt every bump on the road, which rocked his steering and threatened to knock him off his seat.

She was forced to slow when they hit the busy main roads of Holywood, down a tree-lined residential street, passing a bridge. He closed the distance between them as she turned into a housing estate, then braked sharply, forcing him to slam his on and to mount the kerb onto the footpath.

Sonya tried to cut around him, but when that didn't work, she rammed into the back of his bike, forcing him to wrestle it straight. She was behind him now, chasing him, trying to run him down. He swerved in a zigzag, like he'd been taught to do to outmanoeuvre an assailant.

A crash forced him to turn.

She'd hit a wall.

Liam shot off the bike and jogged back towards the car.

Sonya was scrambling to her feet, seemingly unscathed, despite the state of the car's bumper, and the fact that the airbag had gone off, whacking her in the face and sending blood to trickle down her nose.

He ran after her, down the road, right at the bend, coming to the unlit path she'd vanished on.

He could hear the faint smash of waves against the rocks and the howling gusts of wind from the beach below.

'I'm not going to jail,' she called out to him

'There's nowhere else to go.'

She flung a handful of sand into Liam's face.

The salty grains stung his eyes.

She attempted to tackle him to the ground, wrapping her hands round his neck. But he fought one of her hands off his throat and wrenching her hair back managed to pull her down.

Rolling over, he felt a hard blow to the rib but was able to drag her into an oncoming wave as he kicked out to land another.

She turned and started running, splashing her way deeper into the black tide.

The ripples caught the moonlight on the water that was up to Liam's waist.

He caught her by the shoulder.

She tried to break free of his grasp, but the ice-cold sea made tackling her easy.

He thought about his sister, Tina. No one knew they were here. He surveyed the marina, before he tackled her beneath the water and pushed down on her chest.

She struggled but he fought against her, muscles taut, eyes watering as she thrashed about, desperate for air.

CHAPTER TWENTY-THREE

Liam watched the waves smacking against the shore, where he'd dragged Sonya's body.

He was numb, although he shivered. His anger had dissipated, leaving him empty.

He took his phone out of his vest pocket and keyed in the number he knew by heart with shaky fingers.

He sniffed and wiped his eyes with the back of his hand as Carter picked up.

'I need your help,' he said.

'Where are you?'

CHAPTER TWENTY-FOUR

The emergency services had arrived shortly before the police and had taken Ashley to the hospital.

Carter had used the chaos as a distraction to order a taxi to Helen's Bay, where he'd bypassed the wreck of Sonya's car, to find Liam sitting on the sand beside a dark shape that looked distinctly like the washed-up figure of a body.

'What happened?'

'I . . . I . . .'

'You were never here.'

'What?'

Carter stared at the rolling waves.

'You're going to leave here now and let me deal with this. I've been through this circus before.'

'Exactly. They'll have your head for this,' Liam said.

'Get up, turn around and leave,' Carter said, taking out his phone. 'When you're questioned, you were at home soaking in the bath.'

He waited until Liam was out of sight before calling

his boss and telling Paulson he'd pursued Sonya to Helen's Bay.

'I need an ambulance.'

CHAPTER TWENTY-FIVE

TWO WEEKS LATER

Carter entered the hospital clean-shaven and wearing a smile, carrying a large bouquet of flowers in his hand. The sun pierced through the windows and pooled onto the floor of the ward.

He entered Ashley's room following a knock on the door.

'Hey,' Ashley said, beaming. She was sitting up, wearing a big baggy T-shirt.

Carter sat in the chair next to her bed and she tilted her head, indicating the floral arrangement. 'You're not allowed those in here.'

'I'll take them home for myself then.'

Recognising the face on the screen of the television, Carter asked her to turn the volume up.

The news anchor introduced Detective Liam Harding. '. . . who is responsible for closing the case involving The Fisherman, after the suspension of his colleague, pending an investigation by the PSNI into the death of a suspect he was in pursuit of . . .'

***

He didn't stay to listen to the rest. He'd already closed the door on that chapter of his life, both figuratively and literally speaking.

At his feet was a package.

It had been hand delivered through the letterbox while he'd been at the hospital.

He opened it as he walked into the living room. Inside, was the nameplate that had been attached to the door of his office, back at the station. The note that had been folded in half read:

I was going to use it as a doorstop but thought you might prefer to keep it as a memento.

Liam.

Paul McCracken was born in Belfast.

In spring 2011, Paul started to learn the craft of screenwriting and got to work writing his first feature film.

The script would go on to score highly in an international screenplay competition, based out of Los Angeles. It would then place in the quarterfinals of the same competition for the next two years in a row, accompanied by another.

In 2018 he self-published his debut novel, Layla's Song.

In 2020 he secured two book deals with two different English publishers. The first, Where Crows Land, is a detective thriller set in Belfast and published by The Conrad Press (an imprint of Holland House Books), released in December 2020. The Last Rains of Winter is published by PM Books.

Paul currently works as a factory worker and completes his writing in his free time. He is engaged and hopes that his wedding will go ahead this year after multiple postponements due to Covid-19. Paul also has a young daughter and two soon-to-be stepsons.

Love crime fiction as much as we do?

Sign up to our associate's program to be first in line to receive Advance Review Copies of our books, and to win stationary and signed, dedicated editions of our titles during our monthly competitions. Further details on our website: www.darkedgepress.co.uk

Follow @darkedgepress on Facebook, Twitter, and Instagram to stay updated on our latest releases.

Printed in Great Britain
by Amazon

85929078R00107